Power From On High

Studies in 1 Corinthians 12, 13 & 14

A follow up to the series "Scripture Integrity"

Randolph S. Stewart

*All material is copyrighted 2002, 2013 regarding all commercial and unspecified rights

The Studies of Power From On High:

Preface: Why This Series "Power From On High?" — **Page 3**

Study #1: Are All Apostles?: *Seeking to edify the Church.* — **Page 7**

Study #2: To Every Man: The manifestation is given to every man. — **Page 19**

Study #3: Manifestation of the Spirit: All these worketh that one and the selfsame spirit, dividing to every man severally as he will. — **Page 31**

Study #4: Spiritual Things: Gifts, operations, administrations and manifestations. — **Page 48**

Study #5: A More Excellent Way: Faith, Hope, Love- The greatest of these is love. — **Page 62**

Study #6: More That Ye Should Prophesy: Don't stop doing the basics, just prophesy more. — **Page 74**

Study #7: Steadfast, Immovable, Always Abounding: Your labor is not in vain in the Lord. — **Page 105**

Study #8: Power From On High: The profit in manifesting the gift of spirit. — **Page 128**

Preface

Why this series of studies called Power From On High?

Ye shall know...

You have heard the expression, "blind faith?" Blind faith is not a Biblical concept.

...the truth...

In these studies we shall see the truth of what Jesus Christ left for us when he ascended up on high and gave gifts unto men.

...and the truth...

Jesus said, "these signs shall follow them that believe."

He did not say "those that are baptized," "those that acknowledge my existence" or "Those that think I'm a great guy." But to those who believe.

So find out what God had in mind for you when He called you into the fellowship of His Son!

...shall make you free!

Credits

Through the years we at Free Christian Ministry (Lisa & Scott Stewart) have been blessed with the fellowship and teaching of many wonderful Christian believers. As a result we are able to present this class "Power From On High."

As a result of attempting to provide a fresh approach, we will fall terribly short in having any idea as to how, or even when, to credit those upon whose work we've built and who showed us what, and when. For this we sincerely apologize. Understand we've spent many years making this material our own and have looked at everything we are sharing herein a dozen different ways according to the suggestions and advice of literally hundreds of different people via article, sermon, lecture, book, counseling and various other forums for over a two-decade span of time.

We owe specific debts of gratitude to John Lynn and Christian Educational Services for their work of manifestations of holy spirit and the tithe, which we have shamelessly stolen and endeavored to make our own according to our best doctrinal understanding. (John now fellowships with "Truth and Tradition," a great online site, and CES can be found online at Spirit and Truth.). While we today do not see eye to eye on several areas, we thank God for your faith.

Sue Pierce we wish to thank for her work on the tithe and for showing us that "tongues with interpretation" was still prayer, and how it fit with prophesy. We pilfered her understanding as well, and Sue, I still sing in tongues. At the time of the first version of Power From On High, Sue pastored two churches in the Denver Co. area.

And we owe a huge debt to those involved in the Way International from 1979-1987. For from there we realized that the truth inherent in scripture was still ready for the reaping, and though we disagree doctrinally with the Way of those and later years on many issues, most of us were on the straight and narrow road during those years, living in faith, hope, and love. We're sorry for those who weren't and for those who were but were hurt, and earnestly pray you are all finding healing and wholeness.

The idea for this class is fundamentally based on the expansion provided by the Power For Abundant Living Intermediate and Advanced classes by Dr. Victor

Paul Wierwille. Those familiar with that study may recognize some similarities. Again, not deliberate plagiarism, but indicative that this is where we first were exposed to some of these subjects, even if in collecting the wonderful works of those who came before, such as Styles and Bullinger, some error in the aforementioned PFAL was retained or originated. Hopefully we've built past and corrected those errors, and God bless at the resurrection the many people Dr. Wierwille and other teachers in turn "borrowed" from. We owe them as well.

Also we are not without a debt of gratitude to a body of work on all these subjects too numerous to recognize let alone accredit. We are definitely not the only ministry on the forefront of accurately understanding God's Word, nor does our work replace theirs. From the great research institutes to the local Church holding praise services three times a week, each ministry serves its purpose. And the Body of Christ has only one head, Jesus Christ. No man or woman's ministry can embrace and shelter that Body; that is our Lord's job.

This said, we also are not trying to plagiarize anybody's work. All content in Power From On High has been additionally worked according to the best of our scriptural understanding. We hope that the similarities to any other work lay in attention to the teaching of others, common approaches, a common subject, two thousand years of common Christian influence, common beliefs, a common topic of study (the Bible) and a common Spirit guiding our efforts.

To those who have taught us and unknowingly or knowingly contributed, without which not one word of this would have been possible, Thank You.

This, after all, is your legacy as much as it is ours.

"This is a faithful saying, and these things I will that thou affirm constantly, that they which have believed in God might be careful to maintain good works. These things are good and profitable unto men."

Titus 3:8

Study #1: Are All Apostles?
Seeking to edify the Church.

1 Cor. 1:27-31: "Now ye are the body of Christ, and members in particular.

"And God hath set some in the church, first apostles, secondarily prophets, thirdly teachers, after that miracles, then gifts of healings, helps, governments, diversities of tongues.

"Are all apostles? are all prophets? are all teachers? are all workers of miracles?

"Have all the gifts of healing? do all speak with tongues? do all interpret?

"But covet earnestly the best gifts: and yet shew I unto you a more excellent way."

We have come to see this section of Scripture as follows: each fellowship has people good at this, and people good at that, and we strive to get long-term, even lifetime members of our Congregations into such slots.

We have pastors preaching for decades. We have Sunday schoolmarms locked in tight. We have "visiting angels" in "our" Church.

Yet it is God's Church, not ours. (1 Cor. 10:32)

There is absolutely nothing wrong with making sure that in our congregations, there are some who are reading and able to preach, some likewise to visit those too ill to come, some likewise to speak and interpret the prayers in tongues

Remember, though, that this is the structure of the Church. "And God hath set some in the Church..." God sets, not the elders.

Look at 1 Cor. 14:4: "He that speaketh in an unknown tongue edifieth himself; but he that prophesieth edifieth the church." In this section of 1 Corinthians 14, we are talking about "in the Church." This Church is God's Church, and Jesus is the Head. Not ourselves.

1 Cor. 14:12: "Even so ye, forasmuch as ye are zealous of spiritual gifts, seek that ye may excel to the edifying of the church."

Again, this whole section repeatedly points out

that these things take place in the Church. It talks about how we fellowship as a Body when we gather, when we assemble.

1 Cor. 14:18-19: "I thank my God, I speak with tongues more than ye all:

"Yet in the church I had rather speak five words with my understanding, that by my voice I might teach others also, than ten thousand words in an unknown tongue."

In Paul's personal prayer life, he spoke in tongues more than any of them.

But IN THE CHURCH, when gathered in assembly, he knew the priority AT THAT MOMENT was the edifying of the Church.

So, when we are all gathered together, some are set as apostles.

Apostles are sent.

Sent by who? The Bible mentions apostles of Jesus Christ.

Did not Jesus hand pick the first twelve? Did not the eleven go to their Lord to pick a replacement for Judas Iscariot? Did not Jesus handpick Saul of Tarsus, and did he not send Ananias to minister to Saul?

They were each sent to perform certain functions, none of which were necessarily limited in scope by preconceptions of what we think they should have been doing.

God gave gifts to men, including the gift of pnuema hagion, holy spirit.

Jesus too gave gifts, including the ministries of apostles, those who are sent.

Does Jesus still send apostles? I ask you this: is he still Head of the Body?

Not everybody who says "I've seen the Lord" has seen the Lord.

But Jesus does still send handpicked faithful on his missions of grace and mercy. There are still apostles, there are still prophets, there are still gifts of healings, there are still congregations that are more interested in a real relationship with the Lord and in mimicking the way the Church is supposed to be.

And even in congregations where the flock may have strayed, there are those in them that still want to know "the truth, the whole truth, and nothing but the truth."

Thus, as individuals in this Church, we are not supposed to stop with what we have received in the past. We are to "covet earnestly the best gifts."

What is the best gift?

On Christmas morning, for many children in America, Western Europe, and many other parts of the world, the best gift might be a new iPod.

But to some of our children in Congo, a bowl of rice and a day of quiet at the front might be a godsend.

What are the best gifts?

The best gifts are not the most prestigious.

The best gifts are the most necessary, as Paul wrote, "That the Church may receive edifying."

In the Church, at any given assemblage, have all been visited by Jesus to make sure certain things were done? Is everybody going to prophesy? Are all going to heal or be healed?

In a gathering of five hundred, will all teach?

Let's ask another question. Can all five hundred teach? Probably, if all set their minds to it.

But if all five hundred are going about running the meeting, preaching, prophesying, speaking and interpreting tongues, trying to heal each other and work miracles, what do you have?

Confusion.

1 Cor. 14:33 & 40: "For God is not the author of confusion, but of peace, as in all churches of the saints.

"Let all things be done decently and in order."

That includes the ministries of apostles, prophets, teachers, miracle workers, healers, speakers and interpreters of tongues, and the Sunday school teacher.

Does it say "Not all can be apostles. Not all can be prophets"?

No.

We can each be what we need to be, WHEN WE NEED TO BE IT. We should each be what we need to be and do what we need to do.

Paul also said, "I can do all things through Christ who strengthens me." Phil. 4:13

We each can covet the best gifts, which is to say, we are all to rise up and do whatever it is God needs us to do *at any given time*.

In the Friday fellowship we have in one of our homes, we might run the meeting, and then maybe heal a cancer in one of the believers through prayer and faith.

On Sunday morning, we may simply attend the service, then comfort those we mingle with by sharing what happened Friday, and how God can deliver them as well.

You see, a pastor is one who cares for and comforts the flock. Many times in a church the one with the title and the paycheck, as wonderful a teacher he may be, is not the congregation's only, or even perhaps best, pastor.

If you are a believing father or a believing mother you are certainly doing the work of a pastor with your children.

Pray God the man at the pulpit is not the only pastor among hundreds of people.

Friday, at the Bible Study, you are sharing what you have learned in 1 Corinthians.

Monday you are at work or on the subway doing the work of an evangelist, as in chance conversation your dedication to your Lord enters into the talk.

Wednesday, God works through you as you play your instrument in the worship service, and maybe are called on to speak in tongues and interpret.

And every day of the work, you have prayed for and with people, read and shared things from the Bible, encouraged people, treated your children with strong but tender discipline according to the Word of God...

Soon it is Friday again, but the needs of each day may be a little different.

Covet earnestly the best gifts, and yet there is a more excellent way.

He did not say, "there is a better alternative," he was saying, "in addition to this there is a better way. Do this, covet the best gifts, the necessary things, and I will show you the more excellent way in which you are to do these things."

It's all part of the picture, every bit of it.

We each are to "do all things through Christ who strengthens us," and we are to follow through this more excellent way.

1 Cor. 13:1: "Though I speak with the tongues of men and of angels, and have not charity, I am become as sounding brass, or a tinkling cymbal."

You see, Paul writes that if he does not have charity, he is become as sounding brass, or a tinkling cymbal.

Sounding brass, like a chime, and tinkling cymbals sound nice, but the sounding brass is hollow, the cymbal flat.

There is no substance.

Paul says, "I am become."

He does not say the tongues are wrong, or the prophesying.

He says that the error is in him, that he is hollow or flat.

He'll sound real good, he'll sound real religious, but he himself will be spiritually flat or hollow.

In addition to seeking the best gifts, not as an alternative to, but in addition to seeking the best gifts, we are to follow after charity.

It is all part of the package.

And what is this "charity?"

"Charity" is translated from the word "agape," which is another word for "love."

In the Greek were several words for love. We all know "phileo" and "eros." "Agape," in the few secular uses it has been found in previous to the writing of the New Testament, was used altruistically.

Agape love, charity, is not self-seeking. It is the

love behind self-sacrifice, of putting others ahead of one's self.

We put God ahead of us by learning and keeping his word.

We put our Lord ahead of us by seeking to minister to his people.

We put the Body of Christ ahead of ourselves by pouring our hearts and lives out, by seeking the best gifts, and by seeking first to edify the Body in all things we do with the brethren.

It is this charity, this agape love, that will energize the guarding of you heart, and that will energize your fellowship with Jesus the Lord, and with your God, your Father.

Jesus in revelation warns of those that are lukewarm, neither hot nor cold.

He will "spew them out."

If you want to be hot for God, this section in 1 Cor. 12-15 goes a long way in revealing what your lifestyle will look like.

So in the next seven studies in this series "Power

From On High," this is what we will be looking at.

God bless you, and may the Father keep you and your hearts in His agape love as you seek doing His will,

In Jesus' holy name,

Amen.

Study #2: To Every Man
The manifestation is given to every man.

1 Cor. 12:7: "But the manifestation of the Spirit is given to every man to profit withal."

We may look and this and say, "Okay God, I'm ready to do this, but what is it talking about?"

One of the necessary keys in understanding the Word of God, the Bible, the way it was meant by God to be understood is by understanding "To Whom" each part of it is addressed to.

The epistle of 1 Corinthians is addressed to the Christian.

1 Cor. 1:1-3: "Paul called to be an apostle of Jesus Christ through the will of God, and Sosthenes our brother,

"Unto the church of God which is at Corinth, to them that are sanctified in Christ Jesus, called to be saints, with all that in every place call upon the name of Jesus Christ our Lord, both their's and our's:

"Grace be unto you, and peace, from God our Father, and from the Lord Jesus Christ."

See? It is addressed to all who call on the name of Jesus Christ our risen Lord, to the Church of God.

The Church of God does not refer to the denomination by the same name.

It refers to "all that in every place call upon the name of Jesus Christ our Lord, both their's and our's."

It refers to us today, since the Church has not been called into the air to meet the Lord.

This book is to us and for us. It will minister to us, as we cling to its message, "grace...and peace, from God our Father, and from the Lord Jesus Christ."

Toward the end of this book, many people have a hard time understanding this message of grace and peace. We will attempt to get back to it.

Another important key in understanding Scripture is to see how a context develops.

Keeping this in mind, we will take another look at it, to see how it explains itself.

1 Cor. 12:1: "Now concerning spiritual gifts, brethren, I would not have you ignorant."

If you go back and read the first eleven chapters of 1 Corinthians, you find out that most deal with the physical details of life.

In chapter three, we find out that Paul cannot even discuss spiritual things with them. And so we find him correcting their carnal actions, telling them how to live godly in the flesh.

Thus we are all equal in Christ. The only thing that can differentiate is how we walk in Christ. Chapters three and four point out that our carnal works, whether worldly or godly, will be judged.

Chapters five through seven deal much with sexual matters starting with fornication and ending with marriage, but a sidebar regarding using unbelievers to settle our disputes is thrown in there. All these things are carnal matters.

Chapters eight, nine and ten deal with a myriad of physical details, from how we are to behave among the religiousness of the ungodly to how we are to conduct our own rites, with an edict to care for those who preach the gospel in between. Physical matters.

The end of chapter ten and chapter eleven, you might say, deals with our etiquette to others and among ourselves.

But chapter twelve start discussing the spiritual matters.

King James, NIV and many other Bibles translate this first verse of chapter twelve as "spiritual gifts."

But the words "spiritual gifts" are both translated from a single Greek word, "pnuematikos," which means "spiritual things" or "spiritual matters."

You see, all these problems the Church of Corinth was having in the previous chapters dealt with our carnal, our physical actions.

But regarding things of the spirit, Paul would not have us ignorant of.

We are not only supposed to be informed of spiritual gifts, but of all spiritual matters.

You see, spirit is not a physical substance. You might say it is a parallel dimension.

Just like in Star Trek, only real.

Now, every thing pertaining to that realm and every thing pertaining to how it affects the physical realm is a spiritual thing, but not every spiritual thing is a spiritual gift.

The reality of fallen angels, or as we call them today, devils or demons, is a spiritual thing or a spiritual matter, but it is certainly not in the true sense a "gift."

Young's Literal translation for 1 Cor. 12:1 reads "And concerning the spiritual things, brethren, I do not wish you to be ignorant."

You see?

In this section of 1 Corinthians, we move from Paul correcting the Corinthian church for wrong doctrine and practice of physical matters to him correcting the Corinthian church for wrong doctrine and practice of spiritual things.

To do right the Corinthians, and all who call on the name of Jesus Christ, need "not to be ignorant of spiritual things."

When we were not Christians, we had no choice.

1 Cor. 12:2: "Ye know that ye were Gentiles, carried away unto these dumb idols, even as ye were led."

Before we were Christ's, we were dead in trespasses and sin, having no spirit. We were carried to whatever we served, we were led to it.

Whether we worshiped other gods made of wood or metal, or nature, or a philosophy or science, or ourselves, we were led by the world according to our flesh.

1 Cor. 2:14-16: "But the natural man receiveth not the things of the Spirit of God: for they are foolishness unto him: neither can he know them, because they are spiritually discerned.

"But he that is spiritual judgeth all things, yet he himself is judged of no man.

"For who hath known the mind of the Lord, that he may instruct him? but we have the mind of Christ."

You see? Now we have a choice.

1 Cor. 12:3: "Wherefore I give you to understand, that no man speaking by the Spirit of God calleth Jesus accursed: and that no man can say that Jesus is the Lord, but by the Holy Ghost."

Before we were natural. Now we are spiritual.

This is the first spiritual matter Paul pointed out.

1 Cor. 12:4: "Now there are diversities of gifts, but the same Spirit."

Some spiritual things ARE gifts. Salvation, the endowment of pnuema hagion, is definitely a gift. God gives life, it is called "the gift of God" because it is the best gift.

The life of Jesus was a gift. "God so loved He gave," right?

Healing is called a gift, because every time it happens it is a personal gift to that person from God.

Ministries are called gifts to those who are helped.

But every gift of God has the same spiritual force, the power of God, behind it.

They are all done with the same logic, they are all done according to God's Word.

1 Cor. 12:5: "And there are differences of administrations, but the same Lord."

What are these "administrations?"

Eph. 3:2-6 "If ye have heard of the dispensation of the grace of God which is given me to you-ward:

"How that by revelation he made known unto me the mystery; (as I wrote afore in few words,

"Whereby, when ye read, ye may understand my knowledge in the mystery of Christ)

"Which in other ages was not made known unto the sons of men, as it is now revealed unto his holy apostles and prophets by the Spirit;

"That the Gentiles should be fellowheirs, and of the same body, and partakers of his promise in Christ by the gospel:"

The word "dispensation" in verse 2 is the word "oikanomia," and means "administration." The word is used of the administration of a household most commonly, but also of the rule of provinces of a kingdom.

Like the administration of a Presidency, but this is Paul's part in the administration of the Age of Grace that he is referring to.

Think of this whole age as a "province" in the Kingdom of God, and Paul was an administrator, he administered the gospel of the gift of grace through Jesus Christ in his ministry. And his ministry took place and affected the believers in the period of time, the age, of "the grace of God."

1 Cor. 12:6: "And there are diversities of operations, but it is the same God which worketh all in all."

There are diversities, there are many, operations, but God works in all of them.

When the heavens were created, was that the same operation as when a lame man walks or a deaf man hears?

When the fishes and loaves fed the multitude,

was that the same operation as when you accepted the risen Savior as your Lord, and God gave you the gift of pnuema hagion, of holy spirit?

Of course not.

Just as it is you whether you take a step, grasp a pen or solve a problem, it is God that works in all His doings but the "muscles" He flexes may be different.

But there are diverse spiritual operations, and we are not to remain ignorant of them.

1 Cor. 12:7: "But the manifestation of the Spirit is given to every man to profit withal."

When we speak of gifts, administrations, and operations, there have been in the past many ways God has moved. Gifts, administrations, and operations are all differing concepts, each containing facets that also differ one from another.

But in contrast to these many things, THE manifestation of the spirit is given to EVERY man, and as we have read this is addressing "all that in every place call upon the name of Jesus

Christ our Lord."

THE manifestation is given to all who have accepted Jesus as their risen Lord.

Every operation of the spirit that is connected to the physical world affects something in the physical world.

When the Spirit of God pushes around the molecular structure of an arm or leg to heal it, it can be felt and perhaps seen.

When a believer is unscathed by an explosion he is in the midst of, that can be seen.

When the spirit gives utterance to our speaking in tongues, it can be heard.

Felt, seen and heard are "manifestations."

"Manifestations" is in the Greek the word "phaineros," which is related to the word we get "light" from.

The manifestation, the evidence or "glowing" of the spirit is given to every man, so that spiritual operations can result in an evident profit.

When this happens, God is glorified, for it is His mighty hand.

But this is given to every man, to every one of us.

Each of us are to use the spirit we are given in order to make manifest the reality of its presence.

Every one of us has this privilege and responsibility.

Each of us, after all, is filled with the measure of faith.

We each are given this fullness of spirit.

And in the next studies of this book we will explore these truths.

We will find out what these Scriptures in 1 Corinthians tell us that we can and should do. We will no longer be ignorant, but we will manifest the spirit God gave us to the glory of God.

Study #3: Manifestation of the Spirit
All these worketh that one and the selfsame spirit, dividing to every man severally as he will.

To God be the glory, that He chose to work His awesome power through such weak vessels as ourselves.

1 Cor. 12:7: "But the manifestation of the Spirit is given to every man to profit withal."

As we saw before, there are diversities of gifts that God gives to Man, diversities of administrations that rule in the Kingdom of God, diversities of operations when God does various things in this physical world.

It is the same Spirit that provides the power behind the gifts, the same Lord our administrations, our ministries, are centered around, the same God that works the operations.

But God is infinitely creative and able, and thus His abilities, His concern for Mankind, His ways of blessing His creation have been evident in many ways.

Coming out of Egypt, Moses asked Jehovah who should he say sent him.

You see, Moses was Hebrew, but he was raised Egyptian, in the court (and customs) of Egypt.

Egypt had a pantheon of false gods, and each had a "job," each had an ability, and their names either derived from that ability or had become associated with it.

Moses was not only asking God for a name, he was asking God what His job was, what His ability was.

God answered, "And Moses said unto God, Behold, when I come unto the children of Israel, and shall say unto them, The God of your fathers hath sent me unto you; and they shall say to me, What is his name? what shall I say unto them?

"And God said unto Moses, I AM THAT I AM: and he said, Thus shalt thou say unto the children of Israel, I AM hath sent me unto you." (Ex. 3:13-14)

What an odd name that seems to be, especially since after that God goes on in the next verse to say "the master God" (yahweh, or adonai, elohim) has sent Moses.

But God is responding to the scope of Moses' question.

In Egypt, Moses knew Isis was the patron of nature and magic, Horus was the symbol of power, seen as the first pharaoh and the incarnated deity in each ensuing king of Egypt.

God said, I am that I am.

Ehyeh asher ehyeh is the Hebrew.

Literally, it means "I-shall-be what I-shall-be."

In fact, the Amplified Bible translates it as "I AM WHO I AM and WHAT I AM, and I WILL BE WHAT I WILL BE."

God is saying that for His people, He is not just a god of the hills or a god of the plains, a god of healing or a god of prosperity.

He is saying that whatever He needs to do in relation to His people, He will do in accordance to what He has promised.

Diversity of gifts, diversity of administrations, diversity of operations.

"But," 1 Corinthians 12:7 states, "but" in contrast to the diversity, the so-called mysterious ways of God, in contrast the manifestation of the spirit is given to everyone among the Christians.

Every one of us has the ability and the responsibility to manifest the spirit!

What does "manifest" mean?

It means "to make evident."

1 Cor. 12:7-11: "But the manifestation of the Spirit is given to every man to profit withal.

"For to one is given by the Spirit the word of wisdom; to another the word of knowledge by the same Spirit;

"To another faith by the same Spirit; to another the gifts of healing by the same Spirit;

"To another the working of miracles; to another prophecy; to another discerning of spirits; to another divers kinds of tongues; to another the interpretation of tongues:

"But all these worketh that one and the selfsame Spirit, dividing to every man severally as he will."

People have pointed to things in their lives and said "This is how I manifest the spirit: I give to the poor, I comfort the oppressed, I counsel the young."

These are good things, these are things that we are supposed to do. They may even be inspired by the spirit. But these things can also be done without the immediate intervention of spirit.

There are only nine aspects to the way spirit manifests, and we are all to manifest, to use these aspcts. "Gifts of good works" are not listed among these manifestations. Those are some of those physical details Paul addresses elsewhere in 1 and 2 Corinthians. We are all to manifest this spirit, we all are given this spirit.

The first listed is word of wisdom, where God by revelation says how to act in a situation. Then word of knowledge, where God gives information we have no way of knowing by the senses. When these things happen, when these revelations are proven true, that is making evidence the spirit, the spirit is manifest, is "shining" into the world.

Faith that goes beyond what our minds are capable of, to trust God explicitly, to expect the impossible to come to pass just as it does, that brings to pass a witness of the spiritual. Whenever spiritual faith effects the mind of Man, the spiritual and the physical interact, and one of these other manifestations occur as well.

Healings make manifest. Whenever a healing takes place, it is not simply a miracle, although it is a miracle. It is also a gift to the one healed. It is evidence that the spirit has pushed around neutrons, electrons, protons, to restructure or to form pieces of flesh an/or bone to be as it should be.

When a miracle takes place in front of people, does it provide evidence that something spiritual is affecting the physical realm?

Yes.

Israel walked over the dry land across what had just been the Red Sea, which is connected to every main body of water in the world. The water did not just of it's own accord decide to defy gravity.

The spirit somewhere pushed atoms around.

As a result, this activity of the spirit was manifest.

Miracles are evidence, they are proof.

How about prophesy? Prophesy, which is simply saying out what words the spirit puts on your tongue, is the spirit moving to provide the words.

It differs from the ministry of a prophet.

A prophet may prophesy in this sense, one would hope, but a prophet may be called on to reveal things he has learned by revelation.

What is revelation? It is knowledge God reveals that one has no senses way of knowing, it is God revealing what to do about a situation, often when one's logic and senses would conclude other options were best, or would conclude there is no hope. It can also be information regarding the presence or the identity of spiritual life.

In short, what also called in the Word "revelation" is seen more specifically as "word of knowledge," "word of wisdom," or "discerning of spirits."

Discerning of spirits is a manifestation, an evidence that spirit has interacted with the physical realm.

You see, the same operation may manifest in

more than one way, but it will still be seen as one or more of these nine aspects listed of the manifestation of spirit. A healing is also always a miracle, but not all miracles are healings. A healing is also a gift to the one healed. In a miracle, God and the believer are involved, but in healing you may add a third party, the one being healed. Revelation is also needed to know who to heal.

But it is all evidence that the spirit is doing some work, a "manifestation."

Divers kinds of tongues, where a speaker prays in a language of men or of angels and does not himself understand the language is evidence the spirit is giving speech to the person. Interpretation of what has just been said is a manifestation that the spirit has acted, since without this action, the speaker not understanding what he has just prayed in the tongue could not interpret.

These are the only nine ways spirit is seen to work.

Moses parting the sea? What happened?

He could be said to manifest spiritual faith, since any fool knows an ocean doesn't just part so you can walk to the other side.

We are not justified by works, but by the faith we have through Jesus, we will do works.

This faith is a spiritual activity. But if we have it, things will happen.

We will act as we are supposed to, whether it is good works, or believing miracles will happen when God says they are coming.

God also told Moses what was about to happen.

Could Moses have known by his sense what would happen? No. He learned by revelation, which was in that case word of knowledge, and what to do, which was word of wisdom. Would you walk out on a sea bed just because the water receded miraculously? Maybe, maybe not.

God told Moses to lead Israel across.

And obviously a miracle took place.

At least four manifestations can be seen that spirit interfered with natural occurrence.

But that these things can be seen is what it means by "manifestation."

Furthermore, each of these are divided "to every man as he will."

The word "severally" is the word "idios," which means "one's own."

Of course, we are limited to revelation to when God wants to tell us something, and of course to healings and the miracles are as God says "do it.'

But it is as "he, the man," wills. You "will" to accept.

God is not going to have us heal without our active participation, He is not as likely to be giving us revelation on a regular basis if we don't want to be part of it. Or, if we will reject anything He might say because we've convinced ourselves "God doesn't do that anymore."

God gives every one as the individual will.

"But the manifestation of the Spirit is given to every man to profit withal."

It says "manifestation" in the singular. If you have

spirit in you, if you have confessed the risen Jesus Christ as Lord, you have the spirit, the gift of pnuema hagion. Furthermore, this manifestation is given to profit.

"For to one is given by the Spirit the word of wisdom; to another the word of knowledge by the same Spirit;"

People read this and say "For one man...word of wisdom, for another...word of wisdom."

But Moses regarding the parting of the Red Sea was given both the word of wisdom and the word of knowledge. The words "for one," as in "for for one is given" go back to the nearest relative noun.

People go back to the noun "every man" but they miss the word "profit."

This is saying "for to one (profit) is given by the spirit the word of wisdom, for another (profit) the word of wisdom by the same spirit.

Thus, "To another (profit) faith by the same Spirit; to another (profit) the gifts of healing by the same Spirit;

"To another (profit) the working of miracles; to another (profit) prophecy; to another (profit) discerning of spirits; to another (profit) divers kinds of tongues; to another (profit) the interpretation of tongues:

"But all these worketh that one and the selfsame Spirit, dividing to every man severally as he will."

That one and the self-same spirit divides to every man severally (one's own) as the man will.

Again, for a believer to receive revelation from God on a regular basis, as needed and according as conditions dictate, takes participation on the part of the believer.

For God to give the go ahead for the miracles and healings takes participation, takes will, on the part of that believer.

Some of us have seen where unbelievers are around when miracles take place.

Some were convinced and accepted Jesus Christ as Lord, believing the power of God that raised him from death.

They have gone on to serve God and see many

more wonderful things.

Some rejected repentance. They sometimes admitted "something happened," sometimes they simply chalked it up to "trickery" or "illusion."

What other workings of the spirit have they witnessed since then?

A good guess might be "probably zero."

And which of these manifestations are divided to each man as he will?

Well, what do you need at any time?

Faith we need on a regular basis.

Prayer is good continuously, so tongues are good always.

Paul said he spoke in tongues, in his personal prayer life, more than anyone in Corinth.

But in the Church interpretation edifies, and that decently and in order.

How many times is a person going to need a healing?

When we among the sick is a good time for healings, in drastic conditions for miracles.

We read before, "covet earnestly the best gifts," and the best is always that which is needed.

We always need prayer so we should speak in tongues like a house a'fire.

We should indeed be on fire for God so that where we find ourselves, we will be ready to manifest to the nations the spirit we have been given, the gift of God, where ever we may find ourselves.

Eph. 5:1: "Be ye therefore followers of God, as dear children."

God said "I-shall-be."

We are to follow, literally this verse should be translated "imitators," we are to imitate God.

In giving us each the manifestation of spirit for profit, He has made us part of that process.

As we walk in the spirit in obedience, we shall be what we need to be, do what is needed.

We will receive with eagerness what God tells us and act accordingly. We shall believe for the miracles, we shall pray. We shall edify the Church, and we shall walk in faith.

We have seen in these three studies a series of foundational truths that will enable us to more clearly see the rest of 1 Corinthians 12 through 15.

We have set the context, that this entire section deals with spiritual realities.

We have analyzed some key verses regarding spiritual realities such as the manifestation of spirit more clearly. We see that if the spirit is working in our life, we will see specific manifestations.

It has been a lot of work but we are ready to move through the rest of these chapters.

In the end, we will be left with a choice.

Rom. 8:1: "There is therefore now no condemnation to them which are in Christ Jesus, who walk not after the flesh, but after the Spirit."

We are seeing more clearly exactly what it

means to walk not after the flesh, but after the spirit.

Rom. 8:14: "For as many as are led by the Spirit of God, they are the sons of God."

You are seeing more clearly what it means to be led by the spirit.

"Led by the spirit" is not possession. It is will, as you will. It is at every moment a choice.

This makes it a challenge, but brothers and sisters, we have the tools.

Those who are led by the spirit of God are His children.

Does it surprise you He wants to give you knowlege and wisdom, that He wants to speak with you?

Eph. 1:17-19: "That the God of our Lord Jesus Christ, the Father of glory, may give unto you the spirit of wisdom and revelation in the knowledge of him:

"The eyes of your understanding being enlightened; that ye may know what is the hope of his calling, and what the riches of the glory of his inheritance in the saints,

"And what is the exceeding greatness of his power to us-ward who believe, according to the working of his mighty power..."

You are His dear child, called by His name before the foundation of the world. What is this revelation and what is this exceeding great spirit power, but that which when energized is manifest how? That's right, only nine ways.

Let us in the days ahead go deeper into this spiritual truth, and see more clearly what great power has been given to the Church, so that even being weak vessels we can better glorify the Great I Am, He Who has delivered us from this evil world through His Son.

And in so doing, serve the Head of the Church, he who also loved us and set before us the example, the arch-type of the walk in the spirit, Jesus our risen Lord

Amen?

Amen!

Study #4: Spiritual Things
Gifts, operations, administrations and manifestations.

We have seen in the last few studies that after Paul's introduction, the first twelve chapters of Corinthians were written to address error in the physical details of the lives of the Corinthian believers, and to address such things in the lives of all who call on the name of the Lord Jesus Christ.

We have seen that in chapter twelve, this emphasis alters. We are now addressing spiritual things ("pnuematikos" in the text, translated erroneously in 1 Cor. 12:1 as "spiritual gifts.")

We have seen that according to God's design, there are through the ages, or depending on the circumstances, various spiritual gifts, various spiritual administrations, and various operations of spirit.

But that the spirit should be manifested, that is given as the responsibility of each Christian believer, as each believer decides to rise up and magnify God. Now let's look at all three chapters:

I Cor. 12:1-2: "Now concerning spiritual gifts, brethren, I would not have you ignorant.

"Ye know that ye were Gentiles, carried away unto these dumb idols, even as ye were led."

We were Gentiles, ignorant of spiritual realities. We followed every "ism" under Heaven, without knowledge of the God of Heaven.

It is time to grow up.

1 Cor. 12:3: 'Wherefore I give you to understand, that no man speaking by the Spirit of God calleth Jesus accursed: and that no man can say that Jesus is the Lord, but by the Holy Ghost."

Up until the end of the second century A.D., there are records to indicate that the signs and miracles of the Book of Acts were prevalent in the Church. This included the act known variously as "speaking in tongues," "speaking in the spirit," "tongues," or "praying in the spirit."

You are not, as some still say today, "cursing God" by speaking in tongues.

Rather, you are speaking "as the spirit gives you utterance."

Furthermore, no man can say Jesus is Lord but by pnuema hagion, holy spirit, translated here as "the Holy Ghost."

Confess with your mouth Jesus as Lord, believe in your heart God has raised him from the dead, and you shall be saved. "Shall" is absolute.

But to walk as God really would have you walk, you have to start walking in the spirit, doing things that connect your spiritual new life to the flesh of your dead old life. You want to really make Jesus Lord of your life? To not be carnal, like these Corinthians had been? This section tells you how.

It is a package, and part of that package is praying in the spirit.

There are many worldly reasons not to do this, reasons steeped in doubt or unbelief.

There is at least one reason to do this: We are told to.

And this section tells you how to walk correctly in these matters.

1 Cor. 12:4-6: "Now there are diversities of gifts,

but the same Spirit.

"And there are differences of administrations, but the same Lord.

"And there are diversities of operations, but it is the same God which worketh all in all."

Indeed, those actions God keeps to Himself are God's to dole as He sees fit. Indeed, the very "age" we are in now of the Body of Christ was kept a mystery until after it had already started, or else Satan never would have crucified Jesus, and our sins would not have been paid for!

1 Cor. 12:7-11: "But the manifestation of the Spirit is given to every man to profit withal.

"For to one is given by the Spirit the word of wisdom; to another the word of knowledge by the same Spirit;

"To another faith by the same Spirit; to another the gifts of healing by the same Spirit;

"To another the working of miracles; to another prophecy; to another discerning of spirits; to another divers kinds of tongues; to another the interpretation of tongues:

"But all these worketh that one and the selfsame Spirit, dividing to every man severally as he will."

We have seen that God gives out each of these according to as each believer wills. We should see to it that we "will," and walk according to the needs of the brethren.

Keep in mind, these are nine aspects of the manifestation. Manifestation of what? Of spirit.

If the spirit operates in a way that affects the natural order, and the effect of those operations are seen, heard, felt, smelled and/or tasted, i.e., it is manifested one of nine ways.

But we see here how many Christians are taught that a Christian is given one, maybe two or three, according to their own predisposition.

Yet if the deciding factor is how the man, how the believer, wills, then is it not better to say that the deciding factor should be how we rise up and believe God to work in us to do what is necessary AT ANY GIVEN TIME?

If it is available, certainly.

1 Cor. 12:12-14: "For as the body is one, and

hath many members, and all the members of that one body, being many, are one body: so also is Christ.

"For by one Spirit are we all baptized into one body, whether we be Jews or Gentiles, whether we be bond or free; and have been all made to drink into one Spirit.

"For the body is not one member, but many."

No, we are not interchangeable. No, our ministries are not identical.

But we all drink into one spirit. We can all do what is necessary to do WHERE WE ARE AT.

1 Cor. 12:15-17: "If the foot shall say, Because I am not the hand, I am not of the body; is it therefore not of the body?

"And if the ear shall say, Because I am not the eye, I am not of the body; is it therefore not of the body?

"If the whole body were an eye, where were the hearing? If the whole were hearing, where were the smelling?"

Verse 14 of Chapter Twelve starts with the word "for."

It makes this section subordinate to verse eleven, "But all these worketh that one and the selfsame Spirit, dividing to every man severally as he will."

One might say, "Father, I am an ordained minister, but I really feel weird about praying in tongues or interpreting the tongues I speak among the Church. I won't do it."

Another might say, "Carter healed several people again this week, all I got to do was speak in tongues and interpret, or prophesy, at Church."

But Carter was the one there with those healed who had the "will," as in "as he will," when the time was right. Just as the second here was one of the ones who had the will to speak in tongues and interpret or to prophesy when the Church was gathered.

And of course, the one who said "no," regardless of his official status, is one who lacks the will.

Among those of us who have the will, and who act, are we to judge according to what we see? Are we to judge the worth of each manifestation of spirit? No, the only worth is dependent on what is necessary at the time.

1 Cor. 12:18: "But now hath God set the members every one of them in the body, as it hath pleased him."

That's correct. When it comes to this business of manifesting the spirit, God knows what is necessary, doesn't He? That is why we aren't supposed to pick and choose. We need to do whatever is necessary at the time to edify the Body of Christ.

1 Cor. 12:19-22: "And if they were all one member, where were the body?

"But now are they many members, yet but one body.

"And the eye cannot say unto the hand, I have no need of thee: nor again the head to the feet, I have no need of you.

"Nay, much more those members of the body, which seem to be more feeble, are necessary:"

Once again, we are reminded that we need to address the unglamorous jobs as well as the glamorous.

While perhaps not addressing the use of manifestations of the spirit, think of the accounts of Stephen in Acts.

He was set in charge of taking care of widows. Was this your glamour job?

Then he was stoned to death, no reprieve, no angels rescuing him. Glamour?

No.

But there was one in the crowd who heard his preaching, and years later, when Christ appeared to him, Saul believed those words that had laid dormant for years. Saul became the sent apostle who received the great revelation given the Church, the mystery of the grace that we are a part of.

Was Stephen's ministry necessary?

To those widows, wonderful Christian women a part of the Body, certainly.

To the conviction and restoration of Paul, yes.

1 Cor. 12:23-24: "And those members of the body, which we think to be less honourable, upon these we bestow more abundant honour; and our uncomely parts have more abundant comeliness.

"For our comely parts have no need: but God hath tempered the body together, having given more abundant honour to that part which lacked."

Not all jobs are the glamour jobs.

But all of our situations are unique, and so our concern should be to rise up and do what is necessary to minister to the Church at any given time.

1 Cor. 12:25-26: "That there should be no schism in the body; but that the members should have the same care one for another.

"And whether one member suffer, all the members suffer with it; or one member be honoured, all the members rejoice with it."

See? In this spiritual walk, wherein we take care of spiritual things, and manifest the spirit in us, we should have no schism.

We all know what would happen if the intestinal

cells should stop working.

Of course, this is an analogy, and unlike the human body, a "cell" in the Body of Christ isn't always stuck as an intestinal cell. As we do what is necessary, our roles change regularly.

And to those brothers and sisters who want to quit volunteering for jobs in the intestines and become permanent brain cells, we say this: The Body of Christ already has a head, and it is not you.

1 Cor. 12:27-28: "Now ye are the body of Christ, and members in particular."

"And God hath set some in the church, first apostles, secondarily prophets, thirdly teachers, after that miracles, then gifts of healings, helps, governments, diversities of tongues."

Each time you are among the Body, you will be inspired to meet particular functions, you are members in particular.

First come, first served, people. Rise up.

Want to grow?

Grow the Church.

As the Church grows, there will be need for more apostle, more prophets, more teachers and healers.

1 Cor. 12:29-30: "Are all apostles? are all prophets? are all teachers? are all workers of miracles?

"Have all the gifts of healing? do all speak with tongues? do all interpret?"

At any given time, is everybody who comes to church going to be acting as an apostle? Or a prophet? Or a teacher?

Of course not.

At any given time, there may be only a few apostles, a few prophets. There may be only one or two who are teachers on a given Sunday, or whatever days your meetings take place.

1 Cor. 12:31: "But covet earnestly the best gifts: and yet shew I unto you a more excellent way."

Covet earnestly the best gifts.

What are the best gifts?

Answer this: what, in the Church, when it comes to spiritual matters, is the most important thing that doesn't have someone doing it?

What are the most pressing needs of the Church?

Remember, this particular section deals with the ministering to the body broadly regarding spiritual matters, and more specifically it is still dealing with how the spirit is manifested.

What spiritual matters are unattended?

What needs that require spiritual power, and thus will manifest spirit, are not being met?

Covet those things, yet there is a more excellent way.

And this "more excellent way" is not an alternative to coveting these best gifts, it is something that build on them.

It is a way to build, you might say, a life of fulfilling this function so that it becomes first nature for you to actively seek ministering effectively to the Body of Christ.

This "more excellent way" of ministering spiritually to the Body will be our next study in this series in 1 Corinthians 12 through 15.

Study #5: A More Excellent Way
Faith, Hope, Love- The greatest of these is love.

In the very last verse of 1 Corinthians chapter twelve, we are told:

"But covet earnestly the best gifts: and yet shew I unto you a more excellent way."

In these studies of 1 Corinthians 12-15, we are following the Scriptures and are seeing that the reason "the best gifts" are not spelled out here is simply that being best depends on what is needed most at any given time.

We also saw that, while "coveting earnestly the best gifts" or seeking to do what is most necessary at the time may be a wonderful principle for living life, this particular reference directly infers our use of spiritual power in our lives.

At any given time, we are to walk in the spirit as God gives us wisdom and knowledge of Him, and how this will operate at any given time should depend on what is needed most.

Walking in the spirit bears much fruit, but only manifests nine ways. Fruit is not manifestation. We are to be willing to walk so that whichever operation is necessary to bring about the necessary result, we will do our part.

Ergo, covet earnestly the best gifts, the best bestowing of God's grace for each situation, each moment in our lives.

So yes, covet earnestly the best gifts, and yet we will be shown a more excellent way.

"And yet" is not "but." It does not set into contrast. "And yet," as good as you may being doing, there is a crucial aspect to build on what you are already doing.

1 Cor. 13:1: "Though I speak with the tongues of men and of angels, and have not charity, I am become as sounding brass, or a tinkling cymbal."

Signs, miracles and wonders will follow those that believe on the Lord. We shall speak in new tongues, if we are (accidentally or by another's malicious intent) dosed with poison, we shall be unhurt, if we are believing.

Nothing wrong with the tongues, nothing wrong

with all the other stuff. They are aspects of the operation of spirit, of the gift of God.

But if we do these things without charity, we ourselves are as sounding brass, (hollow,) or a tinkling cymbal, which as we know lacks depth.

The tongues are good, but it says we who are doing it are hollow and without true depth.

"Charity" as it is used here is from the Greek word "agape," which is in the profane literature an altruistic selfless love, and in the Bible used to refer to God's selfless love for us.

It is a love willing to sacrifice, willing to serve the interests of those we love.

In the secular Greek literature, "agape" was used so seldom before the New Testament was written that it has only recently been discovered in texts older than the New Testament.

Indeed, most Bible scholars still erroneously believe it was made up to describe God's perfect love, that is how powerful and important it is.

God so loved that He gave, He sacrificed, His only begotten Son, and we are to have that same love.

When we do, our striving to do what at any time is necessary will become so powerful, it will be a more excellent way. We will still walk in the spirit, but with a renewed heart.

1 Cor. 13:2-3: "And though I have the gift of prophecy, and understand all mysteries, and all knowledge; and though I have all faith, so that I could remove mountains, and have not charity, I am nothing.

"And though I bestow all my goods to feed the poor, and though I give my body to be burned, and have not charity, it profiteth me nothing."

Sure, we strive to use prophesy that the Church is edified. We seek and use revelation, and work faith.

But we need to love, we need to surrender our very existence, so that what blesses God and His people, blesses us. Otherwise, we really don't get anything of eternal value from the deal.

Yet God wants us to be blessed in all we do, so He wants us not only to be loved, but to love.

1 Cor. 13:4-6: "Charity suffereth long, and is kind; charity envieth not; charity vaunteth not itself, is not puffed up,

"Doth not behave itself unseemly, seeketh not her own, is not easily provoked, thinketh no evil;

"Rejoiceth not in iniquity, but rejoiceth in the truth;"

We have all seen possessive fools who say they love someone, but are cruel. They say they love, but are full of envy, boasting, pride, ill mannered, selfish, wrath and foul nature.

True agape rejoices not in all these evil things, but in truth.

1 Cor. 13:7: "Beareth all things, believeth all things, hopeth all things, endureth all things."

When you are so filled with love and concern for those you minister to, be they neighbors, friends, family, loved ones, members of the Church, you endure what the Word of God says to endure, trust and act on what the Word says is right, anticipate what God says will come, and keep enduring.

As the song says, "I will fall down, I will stumble, but I shall not be moved."

1 Cor. 13:8-10: "Charity never faileth: but whether there be prophecies, they shall fail; whether there be tongues, they shall cease; whether there be knowledge, it shall vanish away.

"For we know in part, and we prophesy in part.

"But when that which is perfect is come, then that which is in part shall be done away."

How often does this love, this genuine sacrifice of self so that others might benefit of the love of God fail? Never.

All these wonderful tools God gives us, we might find ourselves in bad situations in life, limited not by the spirit in us but by our weakness as being flesh and blood.

Prophesies will fail. When we are resurrected we will have no need of tongues for making intercession. But love will never fail, and it is what it is today same as it is tomorrow: loving others as if they are a part of ourselves.

Knowledge? There will be a time when the

knowledge we receive through revelation will be done away with. We will exist in the same realm as God and His Word shall be written in our hearts, so the knowledge of today will fade away.

Why? Because we shall be spiritual beings in every way, whole, and that which is in part, that which we have today, will be done away with.

But the love, brothers and sisters, the love remains the same.

1 Cor. 13:11-12: "When I was a child, I spake as a child, I understood as a child, I thought as a child: but when I became a man, I put away childish things.

"For now we see through a glass, darkly; but then face to face: now I know in part; but then shall I know even as also I am known."

You see, in our flesh, there was a time when our priorities were the things important to us as children: growing up, playing games silly to us now, learning how to act even.

In the flesh, as adults, we behave in ways we feel are mature. Our priorities have gelled, we seek to fulfill our adult responsibilities, we tend to take maturity for granted in many situations.

But spiritually, we have not reached adulthood. Look at 1 John:

1 John 3:2: "Beloved, now are we the sons of God, and it doth not yet appear what we shall be: but we know that, when he shall appear, we shall be like him; for we shall see him as he is."

We are not face to face yet. When Jesus Christ comes back and appears to us, the Scriptures say the dead will rise incorruptible, and the living among the Church will put on incorruption, because, as 1 John says, we shall be like him.

At that time, tongues will cease for us. We won't be picking up our KJV or our NIV.

But the love won't change.

After the elements melt and God has put together a new heaven and earth, we will have put away childish things.

But it will be the same love.

We certainly will see it brighter, live it better, but love never fails.

And those things we built out of the love of God we will carry with us through eternity.

Those bonds with our brothers and sisters that we built by living love, by sacrificing the things we "felt like" doing so that we could do whatever needed doing, those things are gold, precious stones that will be with us for ever and ever.

Because love never fails.

It is ready to rise to the occasion.

It is the more excellent way.

1 Cor. 13:13: "And now abideth faith, hope, charity, these three; but the greatest of these is charity."

Do we live, do we behave as Christians without faith and hope?

Of course not.

We may have heard those who say, "I don't need to believe for power to come to pass, I don't need prayer that makes intercession, I don't need to understand what it is we call the Rapture. I know

He loves me."

That is like saying, "I'm going to college, I don't need my stomach or my brain, just as long as I have a heart."

It is a package.

The more excellent way is the way of love.

Love tunes you in to the needs of others, and fires up your desire to rise up to do what is needed.

For this reason, its more excellent than only coveting earnestly the best gifts.

You see, walking in love, wanting to do whatever it takes to "get the job done," to deliver and bless God's people, is not a second nature, it becomes your first nature.

It indeed is a more excellent way.

So while it is still necessary to attend to all these spiritual matters, to know of them and act accordingly, it is always to be done in love, which never fails.

While we are to be aware of the rules of the game, the gifts, the administrations, the operations, let's not be motivated basically by what's in it for us.

Sure, Eye hath not seen nor ear heard what God has in store for those who love Him...but its still about loving Him, and His people.

Love, selfless agape love, never fails.

Certainly, we are to walk in the spirit. We are to manifest the spirit in us as God has enabled us according to the needs of each situation we are in, according to the needs of God's people. But it is love that never fails.

And we are to do what is necessary, according not to prestige but according to wisdom from above. We are to covet earnestly those necessary things.

But in addition to that, we are to seek to attain *while doing these things* the more excellent way, that of selfless love according to God's Word.

You see, this section reveals many necessary truths regarding what is called walking in the spirit. But the crux of the spiritual walk is not operating the spirit so that it is manifested, as we are told we can do as we will in 1 Cor. 12:7-11.

The crux of "being spiritual" is not the works we do, but the love we have that motivates us to do these things.

If we are motivated by pride, or by the desire to look good in front of those we love, or by self-interest, those things are still helpful to those ministered to, but we O Lord are hollow and without depth.

Let this not be. Live love.

Now that we have this to keep in mind, now that we are reminded to keep love as our motivation so that we don't go on some "spirituality" kick, now that we have love to keep us grounded, we are ready in the next final studies to explore just how we are to walk in this spirit, how we are to operate spiritually so that the spirit is manifested to the glory of God.

Amen?

Amen!

Study #6: More That Ye Should Prophesy

Don't stop doing the basics, just prophesy more.

In Addition, Prophesy More

In the previous studies on 1 Corinthians 12-15, we have seen that we are not to be ignorant of spiritual things or spiritual matters. We have learned that among these spiritual matters lies the truth that when spirit affects the natural realm, it will be manifest, or "easy to be perceived by the senses," in nine ways, depending on the operation of the spirit taking place.

Speaking of the resurrection, Peter, on the first day of what we often refer to as the Christian Church, had this to say in the very first sermon of this Church:

Acts 2:36: "Therefore let all the house of Israel know assuredly, that God hath made the same Jesus, whom ye have crucified, both Lord and Christ."

Of course, he spake this to many who a few short

weeks before had been instrumental in demanding Jesus was crucified in the first place.

Acts 2:37: "Now when they heard this, they were pricked in their heart, and said unto Peter and to the rest of the apostles, Men and brethren, what shall we do?"

That is a good question. What shall we do? Peter answers.

Acts 2:38-39: "Then Peter said unto them, Repent, and be baptized every one of you in the name of Jesus Christ for the remission of sins, and ye shall receive the gift of the Holy Ghost.

"For the promise is unto you, and to your children, and to all that are afar off, even as many as the LORD our God shall call."

Repent. Romans 10:9 states, "if thou shalt confess with thy mouth the Lord Jesus, and shalt believe in thine heart that God hath raised him from the dead, thou shalt be saved."

Peter had just preached Jesus resurrected, Peter had just preached Jesus as Lord, now he is saying "repent," which literally means, "change your mind about it."

Change your mind. Before you thought, "Jesus died like every other man." Now you change, now you think, "God raised him from the dead."

Before, your opinions were your lord.

Now, you realize that the Lord God has made Jesus lord over all His creation. Jesus is now ruler, and as you accept this truth, you realize that makes Jesus your lord too. That is what confess means, that what you say actually would line up with what is true anyway, whether you accept it or not. But you accept it.

But when you accept that truth, and believe God did raise Jesus from the dead, you are saved, and you receive the "gift of the Holy Ghost."

What is "the gift of the Holy Ghost?"

Peter and the eleven with him had just received the initial outpouring.

Acts 2:4-8: "And they were all filled with the Holy Ghost, and began to speak with other tongues, as the Spirit gave them utterance.

"And there were dwelling at Jerusalem Jews, devout men, out of every nation under heaven.

"Now when this was noised abroad, the multitude came together, and were confounded, because that every man heard them speak in his own language.

"And they were all amazed and marvelled, saying one to another, Behold, are not all these which speak Galileans?

"And how hear we every man in our own tongue, wherein we were born? "

These apostles had already just received this gift of holy spirit, it had filled them.

Now Peter is telling those who have just witnessed this, that they too would receive the gift.

The texts read, "lepsethe ton dorean tou agiou pneumatos."

"Receive the gift the holy spirit."

Brethren, Sisters, the gift is not the Holy Ghost, it is not God. Rather, the gift is holy spirit, a gift to us, life that is created in the image of God.

It is the "spiritual DNA" that makes us the children

of God, Who is The Holy Spirit.

It is the huiothesia, the sonship spirit, incorruptible seed, and it is a gift to us, to as many as the Lord our God shall call.

And when we walk in the spirit, and therefore act in the spirit, these actions are only manifest nine ways.

This section in 1 Corinthians is telling us how to act accordingly in the Church.

We are told to "covet earnestly" the "best gifts," which we have seen is what is necessary at any given time.

We are told that as wonderful as all this is, we are hollow and shallow if we are motivated by anything other than to bless God and to bless the people we minister to.

With these things in mind:

1 Cor. 14:1 "Follow after charity, and desire spiritual gifts, but rather that ye may prophesy."

In this love, desiring spiritual things, this "pnuematika" again, no word for "gift" is used here in the text. But we are to rather prophesy than follow in love or desire spiritual things?

When we think of "rather," we think of a preferable alternative. A choice.

Is prophesy a preferable alternative to love? Not according to the previous chapter. There we see we need the love when we prophesy. And prophesy is a spiritual thing.

What is the apparent confusion?

First, the way this section we are studying is broken up in the English, we forget we are still dealing with the context set in chapter twelve of 1 Corinthians.

There we see that one of the ways spirit is made manifest is prophesy.

We forget we are dealing with the greater context of Corinthians, which is how as a group Christians are to behave.

We think of prophesy, we think of a prophet foretelling something that will happen in the future. Prophesy may well entail that.

But among believers, prophesy as we will see is more likely to be simply words from "the Comforter" of edification, exhortation and comfort, with no word of wisdom, of knowledge or discerning of spirit revelation involved.

This word "rather" is translated wrongly. The Greek word is "mallon," which simply means "more." In fact, it means "to add to" rather than having any connotation of preference.

"But more that ye prophesy."

Don't stop following love and desiring spiritual things and the best gifts. Please keep doing them.

But, more than you are, prophesy. Add prophesy to the tongues you are speaking. Use that manifestation more in the church, among believers.

When To Speak in Tongues

1 Cor. 14:2: "For he that speaketh in an unknown tongue speaketh not unto men, but unto God: for no man understandeth him; howbeit in the spirit he speaketh mysteries."

Remember, this book corrects errors. Among the believers, desire more that you prophesy. Why?

Because if you speak in tongues, you are not speaking to men, but unto God.

In the days of the early church, speaking in tongues was a common, everyday occurrence that all the Christians did. In fact, it was common for believers to speak in tongues until at least the so-called "Great Persecution" near the end of the Second Century AD.

Irenaeus wrote in 177 AD, ""Those who are "perfect" are those who have received the Spirit of God, and who through the Spirit of God do speak in all languages, as he, Himself, used also to speak."

So Paul writes of the nature and use of speaking in tongues. It definitely did not, as scoffers and doubters like to claim, "end with the apostles" or "end when the Bible was finished."

Otherwise we could ignore this whole section.

Speaking in tongues is speaking as the spirit gives utterance, it is speaking in a language that the speaker does not understand. It is not an ability to learn new languages. It is not limited to the few rare occasions like on Pentecost when there were people who understood the languages being spoken of in tongues.

It is speaking in the spirit, i.e. inspiration, unto God, whether anyone around understands or not.

It is, in other words, prayer.

Have you received the spirit of God?

Did you confess Jesus as Lord?

Then you too can speak in tongues.

But here it says that you should more, in the church, desire to prophesy. Why? Because if all you do is speak in tongues, no one will understand you.

1 Cor. 14:3-4: "But he that prophesieth speaketh unto men to edification, and exhortation, and comfort.

"He that speaketh in an unknown tongue edifieth himself; but he that prophesieth edifieth the church."

When we prophesy, we prophesy unto men. Tongues are prayer, up to God.

Prophesy is God to man, and when we are speaking of the believer's prophesy that is listed as a manifestation, it is words that build us. That remind us of what God has already given and promised us. These words exhort us to do what we already know we should do, and it reminds us of what God does to care for our needs.

For example, the song of the prophetess Deborah recorded in Judges ends with "let them that love him be as the sun when he goeth forth in his might."

Did that not encourage and comfort Israel?

Of course.

1 Cor. 14:5: "I would that ye all spake with tongues but rather that ye prophesied: for greater is he that prophesieth than he that speaketh with tongues, except he interpret, that the church may receive edifying."

This word "rather" is again the word "mallon," "more."

Remember the context? This is among the believers.

Paul wanted all them to be speaking in tongues, and we'll find out shortly the ways we are to do this.

But among the believers, "greater," that is, more important when among the believers is he that prophesies so that the Church is edified.

But there is an exception: "Except he interpret, that the Church may be edified."

You see, this is one of the ways we are to speak in tongues in the church, if we speak in tongues and then interpret.

See? It says here "...he that speaketh with tongues, except he interpret..."

See how the man who speaks in tongues also is to interpret?

So many Churches today we see someone speak in a tongue, and then someone else will supposedly give an interpretation.

Why doesn't Paul say here that greater is a

prophesier than a tongues-speaker in the church, unless someone else interprets?

Because that is not how it works. You pray in the tongues, for speaking in tongues is indeed prayer, then you believe God to spew out the same words you have just spoken in a tongue, but in a language that the congregation understands. For most of us, that would be our native tongue.

You pray by speaking in tongues, then you say the same prayer in the language of the people.

You do not understand what you just said in tongues, so the interpretation has to be inspired as well.

Then the Church will be edified. Why won't the Church, the Body, be edified by one of us simply speaking in tongues? Tongues is a tool of prayer, not of missionary work. The exceptions are by grace, not design. Chances are, unless a special circumstance of grace occurs, no one will understand.

Look:

1 Cor. 14:6: "Now, brethren, if I come unto you

speaking with tongues, what shall I profit you, except I shall speak to you either by revelation, or by knowledge, or by prophesying, or by doctrine?"

God may tell one of us to speak in tongues to the assembly without interpreting. Then surely there will be profit, though we may not know what it is.

Or maybe we will know that the context of the meeting allows it. Or maybe, such as on the day of Pentecost, a phenomenon takes place, and to someone of another language, our tongues will be in a language someone in the congregation understands.

Maybe we are simply doing it to give example as we expound on the doctrine regarding the use of tongues.

But these are exceptions, not the rule.

As a rule, we don't simply speak in tongues aloud unless we are going to interpret.

1 Cor. 14:7-12: "And even things without life giving sound, whether pipe or harp, except they give a distinction in the sounds, how shall it be known what is piped or harped?

"For if the trumpet give an uncertain sound, who shall prepare himself to the battle?

"So likewise ye, except ye utter by the tongue words easy to be understood, how shall it be known what is spoken? for ye shall speak into the air."

"There are, it may be, so many kinds of voices in the world, and none of them is without signification.

"Therefore if I know not the meaning of the voice, I shall be unto him that speaketh a barbarian, and he that speaketh shall be a barbarian unto me.

"Even so ye, forasmuch as ye are zealous of spiritual gifts, seek that ye may excel to the edifying of the church."

We are to do things out of love, right? We are to covet the charismata, the grace, that is best for the moment, right?

If you and I simply start to speak in tongues aloud in the Church, as many seem to do even to this day, it will be like music with no rhythm or melody.

If we all simultaneously speak in tongues in the Church, it will be like giving an unfamiliar order in battle. It will be like asking directions from someone who doesn't speak a common language.

1 Cor. 14:13 "Wherefore let him that speaketh in an unknown tongue pray that he may interpret."

There you have it again. He who speaks in a tongue aloud in the Church, outside of the aforementioned and occasional exceptions, is supposed to say the prayer in a tongue to the end that he may interpret the prayer, so that the whole gathering is edified.

1 Cor. 14:14: "For if I pray in an unknown tongue, my spirit prayeth, but my understanding is unfruitful."

See? Speaking in tongues, speaking in the spirit, is prayer.

Why do we need prayer we do not understand? In Romans chapter eight, Paul explains this prayer in the spirit thusly:

Rom. 8:26-27: "Likewise the Spirit also helpeth our infirmities: for we know not what we should pray for as we ought: but the Spirit itself maketh intercession for us with groanings which cannot be uttered.

"And he that searcheth the hearts knoweth what is the mind of the Spirit, because he maketh intercession for the saints according to the will of God."

And so, tongues is a vital prayer tool the Christian has been given as part of the spiritual package, but in the Church, unless interpreted, or used in the aforementioned exceptions, it will not edify.

Knowing this, what then?

1 Cor. 14:15: "What is it then? I will pray with the spirit, and I will pray with the understanding also: I will sing with the spirit, and I will sing with the understanding also."

In the Church, Paul says he will "pray with the spirit, and...will pray with the understanding also."

In other words, he will by speaking in the spirit pray in tongues and interpret the prayer also. He is simply rephrasing the same message over and over again so there can be no mistake, but

Brothers and Sisters, how we have ignored or twisted this simple message as a Church!

Paul also says he will sing with the spirit, and with the understanding also.

What is the context?

Well, every verse in this chapter so far has been about prophesy and/or speaking in tongues, and these verses are specifically about tongues with interpretation.

He will sing in the spirit, which is singing while speaking in tongues, and then he will sing with the understanding also.

In worship, he will manifest tongues and interpretation of tongues as a song!

When Deborah sang in prophesy, was that so much different?

In our worship, are we not told in Ephesians:

Eph. 5:18-20: "And be not drunk with wine, wherein is excess; but be filled with the Spirit;

"Speaking to yourselves in psalms and hymns

and spiritual songs, singing and making melody in your heart to the Lord;

"Giving thanks always for all things unto God and the Father in the name of our Lord Jesus Christ;"

In the first century and a half, this truly and literally inspired singing in the spirit, these "spiritual songs" that were done by singing while manifesting tongues and tongues with interpretation were common.

While careful study of these verses makes it astoundingly crystal clear to us, reference to such a spirit-filled lifestyle were casual in the early Church and in Scripture.

These things were common and they were commonly understood.

So among the believers, if we speak a prayer in tongues he or she who does so needs to interpret. If one sings a prayer in tongues, the same one needs to sing the interpretation.

How much clearer can it be?

1 Cor. 14:16-17: "Else when thou shalt bless with the spirit, how shall he that occupieth the room of

the unlearned say Amen at thy giving of thanks, seeing he understandeth not what thou sayest?"

"For thou verily givest thanks well, but the other is not edified."

See, among other believers, if you speak in tongues, how can he who does not understand the language, who has not learned it, say "Amen" at your prayer, at your giving of thanks?

They simply get nothing from the act of tongues itself. It is as meaningless as if you preached with your understanding in Chinese or Aleut to your typical Kansas farm Church.

1 Cor. 14:18: "I thank my God, I speak with tongues more than ye all:"

Paul wasn't boasting, as is often read. He is simply adding to verse seventeen. Paul also gives thanks by speaking in tongues, in fact, as a statement of fact, he says he spoke in tongues, he thanked God, more than any other individual in Corinth.

Why do you suppose Paul did this?

Because speaking in tongues is prayer that is not

limited by our fleshly believing and understanding. Because there are listed in various verses many wonderful things that speaking in tongues is good for in our own personal prayer life.

But among the believers:

1 Cor. 14:19: "Yet in the church I had rather speak five words with my understanding, that by my voice I might teach others also, than ten thousand words in an unknown tongue."

Paul is clear that simply speaking in tongues in our personal prayer life is great.

Only, in the Church, we need to use it with interpretation so all are edified.

Decently and in Order

1 Cor 14:20-22: "Brethren, be not children in understanding: howbeit in malice be ye children, but in understanding be men.

"In the law it is written, With men of other tongues and other lips will I speak unto this people; and yet for all that will they not hear me, saith the Lord.

"Wherefore tongues are for a sign, not to them that believe, but to them that believe not: but prophesying serveth not for them that believe not, but for them which believe."

Do not think tongues stopped with the apostles, or are seldom mentioned in Scripture. Most of what we are reading in this chapter so far deals with separating the use of tongues in personal prayer and among the believers, where it is as a matter of course interpreted.

Tongues by itself can be a sign, because it is the evidence that something spiritual has taken place. It is a manifestation of the gift of holy spirit. It can even, by charismata grace, be like on Pentecost, where unbelievers heard their own languages spoken by people they knew did not speak them.

As a sign, it can also be rejected.

Many unbelievers both without and within the Church reject tongues as being spiritual.

But to the instructed believers, it's no sign. Those who were saved in the early Church, who had the gift and instructed in its abilities, already spoke in tongues in their own prayer life.

This section is correcting error, right? These believers were walking carnally, not in love like they should have been.

There was great strife.

Paul wants to fix this.

He received revelation of Jesus Christ to do so, therefore it is safe to say Jesus Christ was wanting to correct it also.

1 Cor. 14:23-24: "If therefore the whole church be come together into one place, and all speak with tongues, and there come in those that are unlearned, or unbelievers, will they not say that ye are mad?"

"But if all prophesy, and there come in one that believeth not, or one unlearned, he is convinced of all, he is judged of all:"

Used properly, tongues is a sign to unbelievers. But if all an unbeliever hears is tongues spoken with no rhyme and reason given for it, that person will really wonder about the tongue-speakers.

But if prophesy is used, that same person will think twice about what is being done.

"And thus are the secrets of his heart made manifest; and so falling down on his face he will worship God, and report that God is in you of a truth."

If a person will be reached, prophesy reaches right into truth.

Through our understanding, we do not know exactly what is occurring in the life of a person coming to our spirit-filled worship for the first time.

God does.

The Comforter inside us is tapped into that, tapped directly into all truth.

That is powerful.

1 Cor. 14:26: "How is it then, brethren? when ye come together, every one of you hath a psalm, hath a doctrine, hath a tongue, hath a revelation, hath an interpretation. Let all things be done unto edifying."

Some of us have seen this. "Act any fool way you think is inspired." We enter a fellowship or Church, and people are hootin' and hollerin', falling over, wailing, speaking in tongues whenever they feel like it. Paul says, "How is this? Why are you doing this?

1 Cor. 14:27: "If any man speak in an unknown tongue, let it be by two, or at the most by three, and that by course; and let one interpret."

We need to be respectful and purposeful.

1 Cor. 14:28: "But if there be no interpreter, let him keep silence in the church; and let him speak to himself, and to God."

If there be no interpreter, let him keep silence.

Let him, the one who will not interpret, keep silence.

Brothers, Sisters, we have the package. The only question is, do we have the will? Because remember, God divides as each wills, and we are to covet earnestly, we are to raise up and act on, the best charismata, i.e., that which is necessary at any given time.

1 Cor. 14:29-32: "Let the prophets speak two or three, and let the other judge.

"If any thing be revealed to another that sitteth by, let the first hold his peace.

"For ye may all prophesy one by one, that all may learn, and all may be comforted.

"And the spirits of the prophets are subject to the prophets."

Which prophets?

Ask yourself this: What is the context?

We are dealing here primarily with tongues, tongues with it being interpreted, and more that we should prophesy.

There are persons alive today with the ministry of a prophet in the traditional sense. If the Church was acting more like Acts, and 1 Corinthians 12-14, and Timothy, we would see more.

But we deal here with "more that ye should prophesy."

We do not need everybody speaking in tongues,

everybody interpreting, everybody prophesying at any random time. We choose who will do this and when, or we set a time when someone inspired will do these things, or we have whatever prayer leader or minister is running the meeting pick and choose.

The details we can follow are endless, but the constraints are to as a rule prophesy two or three at a time for the edification to the body, or as we have seen substitute some of that with someone speaking in tongues and interpreting.

God may inspire different things. Maybe a bunch of people are called on to prophesy, or interpret. Maybe you have a meeting where mostly you take turns prophesying or interpreting prayers in tongues.

But these are the guidelines. Why?

1 Cor. 14:33: "For God is not the author of confusion, but of peace, as in all churches of the saints."

1 Cor. 14:34: "Let your women keep silence in the churches: for it is not permitted unto them to speak; but they are commanded to be under

obedience as also saith the law.

"And if they will learn any thing, let them ask their husbands at home: for it is a shame for women to speak in the church."

"Your women."

The women of those doing the prophesying. Rather than disrupting the Church, and trying to pipe in their two cents every time hubby is called on to prophesy, let them bring it up later.

"Honey, that's true, but remember what we did in Cesarea? That was an exception to that..."

No, be silent.

(But are those prophesying always men?

No, those prophesying, even those with the ministry of a prophet are often female.

What then?

Then hubby needs to show the same respect and add the comments in private. For in the Body of Christ, we are one Body, and neither male nor female spiritually.)

1 Cor. 14:36-37: "What? came the word of God out from you? or came it unto you only?

"If any man think himself to be a prophet, or spiritual, let him acknowledge that the things that I write unto you are the commandments of the Lord."

If any man wants to think he is tapped in to the truth of God's Word, let him acknowledge that these things Paul says do are indeed the commandments of the Lord.

Who is our Lord?

Well, who did you have to confess as lord to get saved, to receive the gift of the holy spirit?

That's right, Jesus.

If you want to think you are so right as a Christian, acknowledge these things are the commandments of Jesus.

"...Follow after charity, and desire spiritual gifts, but more that ye may prophesy" is a commandment of the lord.

"I would that ye all spake with tongues but more

that ye prophesied..." is a commandment of the lord.

"Wherefore let him that speaketh in an unknown tongue pray that he may interpret" is a commandment of the lord as much today as it was when written, and will be until we are gathered unto our Lord.

1 Cor. 14:38: "But if any man be ignorant, let him be ignorant."

Someone wants to argue? Fine, let them take it up with our Boss. We just accept what the Word of God reveals, we just accept that Paul wrote "the commandments of the Lord."

1 Cor. 14:39: "Wherefore, brethren, covet to prophesy, and forbid not to speak with tongues."

So many forbid their denominational leaders, if not even their members, to speak in tongues.

Those who insist on speaking in tongues may be scolded, censored, even excommunicated.

Brothers and Sisters, if people choose not to speak in tongues, then that is their business. But God gave us these things so that we could rise above carnal limitations. Let no man forbid us.

1 Cor. 14:40: "Let all things be done decently and in order."

None of these abilities that we manifest of the spirit preempt the other. All of these aspects are simply part of the total package. Remember, "covet earnest the best gift," which is always that which is applicable to any situation, and always walk in love.

The gift of the holy spirit in each of us is a package. We have looked a little in depth of some of the aspects of this package in 1 Corinthians twelve, seen that the epitome of being spiritual is the walk of love, and seen how combining spirituality and love will result in desire to edify the Church.

In the next study of this book, we shall look at a summary of how we became spirit beings, and a look into the future to see what is in store for us at the end of this age.

For this age, the age of the Church of the Body of Christ, shall end, and we shall be gathered together in the clouds to ever be with our Lord, ever basking in his love and grace.

Amen?

AMEN!

Study #7: Steadfast, Immovable, Always Abounding
Your labor is not in vain in the Lord.

In our studies in 1 Corinthians chapters 12-15, we have seen that the essence of these chapters is dealing with spiritual things, with spiritual matters.

Furthermore, we have seen that these matters deal with different spiritual gifts, different spiritual administrations, and different spiritual operations. But the spirit God is put within each of us. We have seen that there are only nine ways this spirit is manifested, that is, evident, in the natural realm.

Chapters 12 and 14 we have seen deal with the way this spirit is to be manifested in individual and in collective worship. This is by speaking in tongues, which is private prayer, and by praying in with interpretation of tongues and by prophesy among the congregation. Most of chapters 12 and 14 deal with these three ways of manifesting the gift of God, holy spirit.

In service to the Body we have seen that there is faith, miracles and gifts of healings which are directly manifested as the spirit is operated. We have seen that in fellowship and communication with God Himself there are manifestations involving revelation. These are word of wisdom, word of knowledge, and discerning of spirit.

Chapter 13 is the meat on the manifestation sandwich, for it is our reason and motivation: the love of God. God loved that He gave, we love and so we serve.

In no way are the spiritual things we have from God or are the things we can do because God enabled us worthless, useless or bad. But we are unprofitable to ourselves if we do not do our works by being motivated by love.

To this end we are told how to behave in order to bless the Body when gathering together, summed by 1 Cor. 14:37-40:

"If any man think himself to be a prophet, or spiritual, let him acknowledge that the things that I write unto you are the commandments of the Lord.

"But if any man be ignorant, let him be ignorant.

"Wherefore, brethren, covet to prophesy, and forbid not to speak with tongues.

"Let all things be done decently and in order."

All this is part of walking in love and acting according to spiritual realities.

Now that we have these things established, chapter 15 of Corinthians continues:

1 Cor. 15:1-2: "Moreover, brethren, I declare unto you the gospel which I preached unto you, which also ye have received, and wherein ye stand;

"By which also ye are saved, if ye keep in memory what I preached unto you, unless ye have believed in vain."

When we are judged by Christ, our works if based on truth shall be rewarded or we will suffer loss, but we ourselves will be saved. But in this life, turning back becomes wholly unprofitable, it becomes empty for us now and at judgment.

1 Cor. 15:3-4: "For I delivered unto you first of all that which I also received, how that Christ died

for our sins according to the scriptures;

"And that he was buried, and that he rose again the third day according to the scriptures:"

The crucifixion and and subsequent resurrection and glory of our Lord is the foundation of our faith. We saw it was what Peter first preached on Pentecost, when the Church of the Body began. Now we see Paul also began with the resurrection.

1 Cor. 15:5-9: "And that he was seen of Cephas, then of the twelve:

"After that, he was seen of above five hundred brethren at once; of whom the greater part remain unto this present, but some are fallen asleep.

"After that, he was seen of James; then of all the apostles.

"And last of all he was seen of me also, as of one born out of due time."

Paul knew these people. They had seen the man they all knew as Jesus alive after he had been buried lifeless in the earth. To them, the resurrection was not a matter of faith. It was fact. Now Paul new it as well, and he was telling others.

1 Cor. 15:9: "For I am the least of the apostles, that am not meet to be called an apostle, because I persecuted the church of God."

If anybody did not deserve salvation, it may have been Paul. But salvation is complete, with no ties to the past save that which we may try to cling to. Why? Because of God's grace and forgiveness.

1 Cor 15:10-11: "But by the grace of God I am what I am: and his grace which was bestowed upon me was not in vain; but I laboured more abundantly than they all: yet not I, but the grace of God which was with me.

"Therefore whether it were I or they, so we preach, and so ye believed."

Paul received and believed, and so did these Corinthians, and so have we that are in the Church today. We believe the spiritual reality today by word and by faith, just as Paul and the others knew by experience.

1 Cor. 15:12: "Now if Christ be preached that he

rose from the dead, how say some among you that there is no resurrection of the dead?"

If the Bible, and therefore the people who wrote it in error, why bother? But there were when Paul wrote this hundreds of living witnesses.

1 Cor. 15:13-17: "But if there be no resurrection of the dead, then is Christ not risen:

"And if Christ be not risen, then is our preaching vain, and your faith is also vain.

"Yea, and we are found false witnesses of God; because we have testified of God that he raised up Christ: whom he raised not up, if so be that the dead rise not.

"For if the dead rise not, then is not Christ raised:

"And if Christ be not raised, your faith is vain; ye are yet in your sins."

You see, then, just as today, people want to pick and choose what they want to accept from the Scriptures. They might say, "Jesus was a holy man, a prophet, but he never rose from the dead. Or even if he did, we won't."

So people were saying that there is no day in which we as Christians will be raised incorruptible, or will be changed to immortality. But either the whole Bible is the truth, or it is packed with lies.

Paul knew.

He had met the Master.

1 Cor. 15:17-20: "And if Christ be not raised, your faith is vain; ye are yet in your sins.

"Then they also which are fallen asleep in Christ are perished.

"If in this life only we have hope in Christ, we are of all men most miserable.

"But now is Christ risen from the dead, and become the firstfruits of them that slept."

You see, when Christ was raised from the dead, all others were granted life in him. Christ is but the firstfruits, the first of the rest of us who will be resurrected. This too is one of these "spiritual matters" that we are indeed not to be ignorant of!

1 Cor. 15:21-23: "For since by man came death,

by man came also the resurrection of the dead.

"For as in Adam all die, even so in Christ shall all be made alive.

"But every man in his own order: Christ the firstfruits; afterward they that are Christ's at his coming."

First Christ was made alive. Then, at his coming, those that are his, those that are saved in him, shall also be raised or changed. This is that which is spoken of when it says in 1 Thessalonians:

1 Thes. 4:14-17: "For if we believe that Jesus died and rose again, even so them also which sleep in Jesus will God bring with him.

"For this we say unto you by the word of the Lord, that we which are alive and remain unto the coming of the Lord shall not prevent them which are asleep.

"For the Lord himself shall descend from heaven with a shout, with the voice of the archangel, and with the trump of God: and the dead in Christ shall rise first:

"Then we which are alive and remain shall be caught up together with them in the clouds, to meet the Lord in the air: and so shall we ever be with the Lord."

So the dead in Christ and those who are alive in him shall be gathered upon Christ's coming, to meet him in the air.

When Christ returns, we do not have to worry about following a fake.

If he's the real Jesus, we'll notice a change in us we've never noticed before: a new body that has the ability to fly.

Hard for a false Jesus to fake that one.

1 Cor. 15:24-16: "Then cometh the end, when he shall have delivered up the kingdom to God, even the Father; when he shall have put down all rule and all authority and power.

"For he must reign, till he hath put all enemies under his feet.

"The last enemy that shall be destroyed is death."

Christ shall reign until the end. When the end

comes, he will take the kingdom God gave him and give it back to God.

At that time, a last enemy shall be destroyed: death.

People call death "the way back to God."

Baloney. Death is an enemy. It is the scourge by he who has the power of death, the devil.

The devil is a bad one, and so is death.

It is an enemy.

1 Cor. 15:27: "For he hath put all things under his feet. But when he saith all things are put under him, it is manifest that he is excepted, which did put all things under him."

God put all things under Jesus' feet except Himself. That is obvious, or as phrased here, "manifest."

1 Cor. 15:28: "And when all things shall be subdued unto him, then shall the Son also himself be subject unto him that put all things under him, that God may be all in all."

This is the true "returning to God," when death is defeated and God is given back the dominion He gave to Adam that was re-won by Jesus. All things will then be as they should be.

1 Cor. 15:29: "Else what shall they do which are baptized for the dead, if the dead rise not at all? why are they then baptized for the dead?"

But if the dead do not raise, then it is all baloney.

1 Cor. 15:30: "And why stand we in jeopardy every hour?"

If Christ is not raised, if we will not be raised in him, it is all for nought. Why bother? Those claiming to stand as Christians but who do not preach the resurrection are preaching nonsense.

1 Cor. 15:31-32: "I protest by your rejoicing which I have in Christ Jesus our Lord, I die daily.

"If after the manner of men I have fought with beasts at Ephesus, what advantageth it me, if the dead rise not? let us eat and drink; for to morrow we die."

The Young's Literal Translation of these verses makes more sense:

1 Cor. 15:29-32: "Seeing what shall they do who are baptized for the dead, if the dead do not rise at all? why also are they baptized for the dead?

"why also do we stand in peril every hour?

"Every day do I die, by the glorying of you that I have in Christ Jesus our Lord:

"if after the manner of a man with wild beasts I fought in Ephesus, what the advantage to me if the dead do not rise? let us eat and drink, for tomorrow we die!"

If the dead do not rise, why do we sacrifice so much to fight for a doctrine that is not based in reality? Better to bother about the things of this life, for then tomorrow we die!

We do bother about these things because we know God's words are true! Of the spiritual matters revealed to us, they all pivot on the reality that God raised Jesus from the dead. If we reject the resurrection, then in reality, we reject the truth entirely.

1 Cor. 15:33-34: "Be not deceived: evil communications corrupt good manners.

"Awake to righteousness, and sin not; for some have not the knowledge of God: I speak this to your shame."

To deny the resurrection is to communicate with evil, it is to sin.

2 Tim 2:18: "Who concerning the truth have erred, saying that the resurrection is past already; and overthrow the faith of some."

To pretend Christian faith while denying the resurrection is to err, it is to communicate with corruption, it is to overthrow the faith of some.

1 Cor. 15:35-39: "But some man will say, How are the dead raised up? and with what body do they come?

"Thou fool, that which thou sowest is not quickened, except it die:

"And that which thou sowest, thou sowest not that body that shall be, but bare grain, it may chance of wheat, or of some other grain:

"But God giveth it a body as it hath pleased him, and to every seed his own body.

"All flesh is not the same flesh: but there is one kind of flesh of men, another flesh of beasts, another of fishes, and another of birds."

You see, similarities and differences of animal and vegetative life is not the result of some evolutionary lottery. These variations are by godly design, that each creature serves the purposes of God.

1 Cor. 15:40-42: "There are also celestial bodies, and bodies terrestrial: but the glory of the celestial is one, and the glory of the terrestrial is another.

"There is one glory of the sun, and another glory of the moon, and another glory of the stars: for one star differeth from another star in glory.

"So also is the resurrection of the dead. It is sown in corruption; it is raised in incorruption:"

Heavenly bodies also vary. The sun, the stars, the moon, are all glorious in different ways.

The stars dazzle the night sky, while the moon, less than the least of these stars, rules it above all the stars by reflecting the sun.

And the sun rules the day directly just as the moon rules the night, and does not the sun rule the night as well, by reflecting its light on the moon? Just like God rules the darkness of these ages by reflecting His light through Jesus.

So it is that each body differs in what it is and what its for. God did not alter this pattern creating spiritual bodies. Or as should be said, the pattern used in creating spiritual life continued when He created physical life.

1 Cor. 15:42-45: "So also is the resurrection of the dead. It is sown in corruption; it is raised in incorruption:

"It is sown in dishonour; it is raised in glory: it is sown in weakness; it is raised in power:

"It is sown a natural body; it is raised a spiritual body. There is a natural body, and there is a spiritual body.

"And so it is written, The first man Adam was made a living soul; the last Adam was made a quickening spirit."

Adam was made a living soul. Jesus was made a quickening, a life giving, spirit.

1 Cor. 15:46-48: "Howbeit that was not first which is spiritual, but that which is natural; and afterward that which is spiritual.

"The first man is of the earth, earthy; the second man is the Lord from heaven."

"As is the earthy, such are they also that are earthy: and as is the heavenly, such are they also that are heavenly."

As Adam was natural, dead spiritually in trespasses and sin, so are men born of women. As Jesus is spiritual, those born of God's spirit, those with the gift of the holy spirit, are created spiritual.

1 Cor. 15:49: "And as we have borne the image of the earthy, we shall also bear the image of the heavenly."

We also started dead in trespasses and sin, carnal, without spiritual life. God put His seed, His spiritual image in us when we accepted the risen Jesus as Lord and were born again. Therefore:

1 Cor. 15:50: "Now this I say, brethren, that flesh and blood cannot inherit the kingdom of God;

neither doth corruption inherit incorruption."

That's so true. Our dead carnal life could not inherit spiritual rewards, our carnal bodies could not inherit life eternal.

1 Cor. 15:51-53: "Behold, I shew you a mystery; We shall not all sleep, but we shall all be changed,

"In a moment, in the twinkling of an eye, at the last trump: for the trumpet shall sound, and the dead shall be raised incorruptible, and we shall be changed.

"For this corruptible must put on incorruption, and this mortal must put on immortality."

A "mystery" in Scripture is not a secret, even though the "great mystery" had been secret. A "mystery" in Scripture is something revealed to the initiated. Rest assured: It will happen just like it says here and in 1 Thessalonians.

1 Cor. 15:54: "So when this corruptible shall have put on incorruption, and this mortal shall have put on immortality, then shall be brought to pass the saying that is written, Death is swallowed up in victory.'

Death is an enemy, remember? God doesn't kill someone "so he can have another rose petal in Heaven," as is read in many a eulogy. Rather, we are comforted that Jesus will come and those we love will be raised from death.

Psalm 6:5: "For in death there is no remembrance of thee: in the grave who shall give thee thanks?"

We will need to be resurrected if we die because we are dead. We will not be in Heaven with our Lord, waiting for him to come back with us. We will be dead, with no conscious thought, awaiting his return for us. The dead are dead.

So the dead in Christ, like everybody else, will need to be resurrected.

To teach the resurrection has already happened or that there will be no resurrection is to err, it is to teach evil communication, it is to overthrow the faith of those that believe the lie.

Our victory is when we are raised to meet the Lord in the air. The final defeat of the enemy death will be when all things are brought back into obedience to God at the end.

Therefore,

"O death, where is thy sting? O grave, where is thy victory?

"The sting of death is sin; and the strength of sin is the law.

"But thanks be to God, which giveth us the victory through our Lord Jesus Christ." 1 Cor. 15:55-57

See? It is through this resurrection, through this victory we have courtesy of Jesus Christ our Lord, that God gives us the victory over our enemy Death.

What then?

1 Cor. 15:58: "Therefore, my beloved brethren, be ye stedfast, unmoveable, always abounding in the work of the Lord, forasmuch as ye know that your labour is not in vain in the Lord."

No, brothers and sisters, our labors are not wasted.

As we walk in newness of life, mindful of spiritual realities, and walking in godliness through obedience to God's Word and to our Lord Jesus

Christ, our treasures are laid in waiting for the victory of the resurrection.

Because we have eternal life, let us be steadfast, always abounding in the work of the Lord.

What work is this?

It is spiritual work, done in the love of God.

It is ministering work, bringing spiritual wholeness to those who receive our word.

It is faith to bring faith to the weak, healing to the hurt, life to the spiritually dead.

It is to minister miracles to the helpless, it is to have faith in that which is beyond carnal comprehension, it is to minister healing to those who have been broken.

It is to receive at God's discretion but by our willing and ready minds God's wisdom, His knowledge, and God's awareness of the presence and identity of spirit so that we can free the oppressed and act according to spiritual realities.

These are the labors that we are told to abound

in, so that God Who is Spirit is glorified now and in the ages to come, and so that the world can truly know that God so loved the world, that He gave His only begotten Son so that we can shine as lights, as spiritual beings, in the dead and needy world.

These are the labors we are told we can undertake, because brethren, now, right now we are the children of the Most High, brothers of the Lord Christ who is with us and who strengthens our hands to the task.

We are born to live, we are born again to serve.

These abilities are not given to make us proud or superior to our fellow man. They are given so that, like our Lord before us and in whose name we speak, we can better serve.

These are the clear truths of this section of 1 Corinthians 12 through 15.

In concluding this series of studies we will have a final study on the manifestation of spirit in the senses realm as outlined in 1 Corinthians 12:7-11.

After all, the manifestation of spirit is simply the

how or the way spirit is made evident by the effect it has on the material, physical world it effects.

As we have seen, this section we have studied deals in depth with the way the Church is to come together.

So the emphasis here in chapters twelve and fourteen has been on the manifestations that are conducive to worship in the Church.

Chapter fourteen concentrates on speaking and interpreting tongues and prophesy. The former is prayer to God in the spirit among the faithful which builds faith, the latter is the inspired messages to the gathered believers from the spirit that can edify, comfort and exhort the Church to stand on what it has seen to do.

But the gathering of the faithful is only one context in which the spiritual reality of the operation of spirit can be found in. So our final study of this exploration of this section of 1 Corinthians will concentrate on the nine ways the working of spirit is made manifest or evident to us.

It is then hoped that, armed with this information, we may be more mature children for the God Who called us to His household.

That we may be more dutiful servants to the Lord who redeemed us.

That we may be more effective ministers to the men and women within and without the Church, who need us to be at our very best representing the name of Christ.

Amen?

Amen!

Study #8: Power From On High
The profit in manifesting the gift of spirit.

Thank you so much for staying with us during this long and complex study of 1 Corinthians chapters 12-15. As you have seen, even a cursory yet accurate understanding entails so much more than these few chapters. You need a familiarity with what was given to the Church after Jesus ascended and sent the Comforter.

Indeed, we have barely scratched the surface of what the early Church knew it had.

Yet while trying to get to the intended meaning of this section, we have found that once we get to the bottom, the entire section is simple and fits together. It makes sense from the first verse to the last, and contains a single train of subject matter and logic.

Bear with us one more time.

In our recent studies of 1 Corinthians chapters 12 through 15, we have found that these chapters deal extensively with spiritual matters as they take place in the gathering of believers.

Some of the spiritual matters we are not to be ignorant of involve gifts from God, administrations of earth within the Kingdom of God (for it is all God's reign) and ways spirit operates.

But we find that much of these chapters concentrate on what is called "manifestation of spirit."

1 Cor. 12:7-11: "But the manifestation of the Spirit is given to every man to profit withal.

"For to one is given by the Spirit the word of wisdom; to another the word of knowledge by the same Spirit;

"To another faith by the same Spirit; to another the gifts of healing by the same Spirit;

"To another the working of miracles; to another prophecy; to another discerning of spirits; to another divers kinds of tongues; to another the interpretation of tongues:

"But all these worketh that one and the selfsame

Spirit, dividing to every man severally as he will. "

"Manifestation" means evidence.

Whenever spirit interacts with the material world, something takes place in the material realm that can either be seen, or heard, or smelled, or felt, even tasted, or various combinations of the above.

For example, when the blind were healed in the Gospels, they could see the difference. Others, too, could see that the men were no longer poking along blindly.

They could not see the way spirit pushed around the molecules that made up the eyes or optic nerves of those men. But something might have been felt as the healing took place.

Who knows, maybe a little "pop" happened when matter was rearranged?

The unseen action of spirit was manifest, evident, in the material realm.

Revelation, word of wisdom, word of knowledge, discerning of spirit might be heard, or in the case of a Babylonian king who saw writing on the wall, seen. But spirit moves and our world is affected. Again, t he unseen action of spirit was manifest, evident, in the material realm.

When a believer speaks in tongues, that can be heard. The operation of the spirit makes a measurable change that is manifested in the senses realm.

Speaking in tongues? What is that?

Mark 16:14-19: "Afterward he appeared unto the eleven as they sat at meat, and upbraided them with their unbelief and hardness of heart, because they believed not them which had seen him after he was risen.

"And he said unto them, Go ye into all the world, and preach the gospel to every creature.

"He that believeth and is baptized shall be saved; but he that believeth not shall be damned.

"And these signs shall follow them that believe; In my name shall they cast out devils; they shall speak with new tongues;

"They shall take up serpents; and if they drink any deadly thing, it shall not hurt them; they shall lay hands on the sick, and they shall recover.

"So then after the Lord had spoken unto them, he was received up into heaven, and sat on the right hand of God."

Much of the last things Jesus said before he was taken up entailed something called "power from on high" and "the gift of the holy spirit."

Here Jesus listed casting out devils, speaking in tongues, immunity from toxins and poisons and gifts of healings. These are all lumped as aspects of the "manifestation" of spirit in 1 Corinthians 12:7.

Acts 2:1-4: "And when the day of Pentecost was fully come, they were all with one accord in one place.

"And suddenly there came a sound from heaven as of a rushing mighty wind, and it filled all the house where they were sitting.

"And there appeared unto them cloven tongues like as of fire, and it sat upon each of them.

"And they were all filled with the Holy Ghost, and began to speak with other tongues, as the Spirit gave them utterance."

This day of Pentecost was fifty days after the resurrection, perhaps ten days after the ascension.

These apostles were told to wait for the gift, but now it has been given. We do not have to wait any more.

Acts 10:44-46a: "While Peter yet spake these words, the Holy Ghost fell on all them which heard the word.

"And they of the circumcision which believed were astonished, as many as came with Peter, because that on the Gentiles also was poured out the gift of the Holy Ghost.

"For they heard them speak with tongues, and magnify God."

You see, in the early years of the Church, speaking in tongues was the normal thing to do in the Church. People who don't want to believe deny it and say these evidences of the spirit, this "power from on high," ceased with the apostles.

But as late as 177 AD, this was said of the Christians in "Against Heresies:"

"Christians still heal the blind, deaf, and chase away all sorts of demons. Occasionally the dead are raised...

"Some Christians do certainly and truly drive out devils, so that those who have thus been cleansed from evil spirits frequently both believe in Christ, and join themselves to the Church. Others have foreknowledge of things to come: they see visions, and utter prophetic expressions. Others still, heal the sick by laying their hands upon them, and they are made whole. Yea, moreover, as I have said, the dead even have been raised up, and remained among us for many years. The Church does not perform anything by means of angelic invocations, or incantations, or by any other wicked curious art; but, directing her prayers to the Lord...

"Those who are "perfect" are those who have received the Spirit of God, and who through the Spirit of God do speak in all languages, as he, Himself, used also to speak. In like manner we do also hear many brethren in the Church, who possess prophetic gifts, and who through the Spirit speak all kinds of languages, and bring to light for the general benefit the hidden things of men, and declare the mysteries of God, whom also the apostle terms "spiritual," they being spiritual because they partake of the Spirit, and seek spiritual understanding to become purely spiritual..."

Irenaeus, 177, Against Heresies

The dead are raised and remain many years? This is a century after the last of the original apostles, and Paul, have passed. But we see that the power from on high did not stop either with the apostles, or with the Book of Revelation, as many today claim.

Those who claim the finished Bible or the deaths of the Apostles signaled the ends of these things are liars.

Maybe their intentions are good, but they are in error, just as Paul was when he was persecuting the Church. They perpetuate a great lie.

In these studies, we have dealt with the verses

that appear to say that speaking in tongues is wrong or at best, unnecessary. We have seen that there is nothing wrong with the speaking in tongues, it is us using them at the wrong time or not out of a good motivation.

We are told that when this happens, we are to change the way we speak in tongues, not that we do it in the first place.

Luke 24:49: "And, behold, I send the promise of my Father upon you: but tarry ye in the city of Jerusalem, until ye be endued with power from on high."

Again, much of what Jesus said just before he ascended dealt with receiving this power from on high, this gift.

On the Day of Pentecost that was the "birth" of the new Church, Peter's sermon tells the people who heard the initial outpouring this:

"Then Peter said unto them, Repent, and be baptized every one of you in the name of Jesus Christ for the remission of sins, and ye shall receive the gift of the Holy Ghost.

"For the promise is unto you, and to your children, and to all that are afar off, even as many as the LORD our God shall call." Acts 2:38-39

This promise, this same gift of "pnuema hagion" as it is called in the text, is to all who are called.

Have you been called? Are you responding to the whispering voice of your Lord, Jesus Christ

Then this gift is yours.

Confess Jesus as Lord, believe in your heart God raised him from the dead, and you shall be saved.

That is the promise.

And if you are saved, you can speak in tongues at will, you can interpret what you have just said, you can prophesy to the edifying of the Church.

Are you less saved if you decide not to do these things?

No.

Confess Jesus as Lord, believe God raised him, saved, that is the promise.

You might park your shiny new Lincoln in the garage and show up to your executive meeting in the barely-running, rusty Ford Galaxy that was the first car Mommy and Daddy gave you while you were starting college way back when.

Why would you want to?

You can speak in tongues, interpret, prophesy.

You can receive word of wisdom, word of knowledge, discerning of spirit.

You can act on spiritual faith, work miracles, minister gifts of healings.

You can do these things, if you are born again.

Faith as a manifestation is seen when one of the promises of God comes to pass, that could have no logical natural explanation.

Faith is not dead. While it does not come from works, it will result in them. Jesus said, "These signs shall follow them that believe."

James said "Faith without works is dead," and brethren, how we of the Church have been robbed by the thief of so much we have available.

"Lord, I believe, help me my unbelief."

That is faith filling the gap, a spirit-based trust and expectation of the promises of God.

Miracles and gifts of healing are not magic.

You do not "cast a spell" and get what you want.

Exodus 14-13-15: "And Moses said unto the people, Fear ye not, stand still, and see the salvation of the LORD, which he will shew to you to day: for the Egyptians whom ye have seen to day, ye shall see them again no more for ever.

"The LORD shall fight for you, and ye shall hold your peace.

"And the LORD said unto Moses, Wherefore criest thou unto me? speak unto the children of Israel, that they go forward:"

Look at Moses. His idea was, Israel, stand still, the Lord will fight for you."

Well, that seems like his only option, and sure he was trusting in Jehovah.

But the LORD said, "Wherefore criest after me?" Where did you, Moses, get the idea that was what I was going to do?

Obviously, Moses put his own words in his mouth and tried to get God to honor them, like a magic spell.

God was literally sarcastic.

Hint: He is God and knows what He plans on doing; We are NOT God and don't know what WE plan on doing half the time, let alone all the methods He may devise.

Moral: Wait for God to tell you what He plans on doing before you say He's going to do it.

Of course, God covered for Moses, not to embarrass him, as He was the One Who got Moses involved in the first place. You start acting on the promises already given in Scripture, you'll find a lot of grace too.

Just remember that God decides when He speaks.

Word of wisdom, word of knowledge, discerning

of spirit.

There are actually different operations that might result in this.

God may send an angel as He did with the burning bush to Moses or the speaking ass to Balaam.

And surely much of our wisdom and understanding of Scripture is the "still, small voice" of the Comforter, which also whispers in our interaction with this world.

Jesus discerned devil spirits quite often as a foul smell. God knows what He wants to say, and how He can best say it. How He will speak with you most depends on you, but it will NEVER contradict what has been written in Scripture.

Scripture remains our rulebook, our standard of what's true or not.

All these different operations of unseen spirit are "manifest" in one or more of nine ways described by 1 Corinthians 12:7-11. Some of these will manifest after operations we trigger by our actions, because we ourselves operate the mechanics of tongues, interpretation of tongues and prophesy.

The rest are like this event in Exodus, all subject to God deciding what He wants to do. Moses has a plan of his own, but God corrects him.

Here, Moses hears God audibly:

"Speak unto the children of Israel, that they go forward:"

Knowledge can best be described as "the facts."

Wisdom can best be described as "what action to take according to the facts."

The Lord has not revealed why Moses is to tell Israel to go forward, when there is a huge sea standing between them and the closest dry land in that direction, miles away.

But it is still revelation of a "word of wisdom."

The best any man can tell you about "manifesting" revelation is serve God, obey His Word, act on what you know to do, and when He has something to say to you, you'll be the first to know. Then act on it according to what He tells you.

Revelation is not a conjuring up. The power of God is not magic. It is you being on the receiving end of a two-way conversation with the Almighty.

Just don't push Him. Don't worry. Keep ministering via a walk in the spirit. You'll end up in situations where your only way through is for God to tell you what you don't know. Like Moses, who had just told Israel to stand and wait for the Egyptian army, who had the express purpose of severely shortening their freedom and their lives.

Word of wisdom can come first, before word of knowledge.

In other situations, word of wisdom may not be the first thing God tells you, but often it is. Once you recognize His voice, you should know you can trust it no matter how badly you seem trapped by the world.

If you do not know all the knowledge, the wisdom might seem foolish, like marching toward the Red Sea must have seemed foolish to Israel. It will not be. God has a plan.

Ex. 14:16-18: "But lift thou up thy rod, and stretch out thine hand over the sea, and divide it: and the children of Israel shall go on dry ground through the midst of the sea.

"And I, behold, I will harden the hearts of the Egyptians, and they shall follow them: and I will get me honour upon Pharaoh, and upon all his host, upon his chariots, and upon his horsemen.

"And the Egyptians shall know that I am the LORD, when I have gotten me honour upon Pharaoh, upon his chariots, and upon his horsemen."

Moses may have started arguing with God as soon as the Lord told him to tell Israel to march into the sea. He may have said, "Lord, we'll drown."

But by now, Moses had learned to trust God.

If we were smart enough to figure all things out, God would not have to tell us things.

Moses heard revelation, first what to do, which is "word of wisdom." When God offers a suggested course of action, do yourself a favor. Consider it a command, and just do it.

Then he was told the facts about this course of action, including some foretelling. This was word of knowledge.

There are no percentage rules that tell you exactly what to do to receive these revelations, only that you need to learn to act. As you minister in faith, these things shall be provided as necessary. God works with those who work for Him.

God will be what He needs to be, remember?

Act, walk in faith.

Notice what happens AFTER Moses acts on the word of wisdom:

Ex. 14:22: "And Moses stretched out his hand over the sea; and the LORD caused the sea to go back by a strong east wind all that night, and made the sea dry land, and the waters were divided."

You see, whether miracles or gifts of healings (which are just miracles when another's faith is involved as yours is,) first you find out the promise of God, then you act on it.

The promise of God to Moses was deliverance. The word of wisdom to receive what God had already promised, to get deliverance, was "tell them to go forth."

Moses acted, and God did the hard part.

Acts 3:11-12: "And as the lame man which was healed held Peter and John, all the people ran together unto them in the porch that is called Solomon's, greatly wondering.

"And when Peter saw it, he answered unto the people, Ye men of Israel, why marvel ye at this? or why look ye so earnestly on us, as though by our own power or holiness we had made this man to walk?"

See? The worship of tongues, interpretation and prophesy that we control is available through the gift of God, part of our conversing with God. The word of knowledge, of wisdom, the discerning of spirit is simply God, of His own volition, conversing with us.

(Of course, God sends messenger spirits as well, at which times the spirit interacting with the material realm is the angel, and the spirit that is manifest is the angel.

The realm of darkness works the same way, but that is beyond the scope of this study.)

Then God acts on His promises when we obey what we are told to do to receive them.

How simple is that?

But in this day, we have been given holy spirit, we have been given power from on high.

Rom. 8:1: "There is therefore now no condemnation to them which are in Christ Jesus, who walk not after the flesh, but after the Spirit."

Brothers and sisters, we do not HAVE to speak in tongues, interpret or prophesy. These things are only done as we will.

And the genuine manifestations are subject to our will; not that they will happen, but "if."

If a man or woman seeks to not manifest spirit,

why, God will honor that. But that will then be what you can expect when it comes to revelation and power.

Look at this:

Jude 1:17-21: "But, beloved, remember ye the words which were spoken before of the apostles of our Lord Jesus Christ;

"How that they told you there should be mockers in the last time, who should walk after their own ungodly lusts.

"These be they who separate themselves, sensual, having not the Spirit.

"But ye, beloved, building up yourselves on your most holy faith, praying in the Holy Ghost,

"Keep yourselves in the love of God, looking for the mercy of our Lord Jesus Christ unto eternal life."

Of course, remember, we are to keep ourselves in the love of God.

But those who walk after their own lusts, after

their own desires, are those who have not the spirit.

Without the spirit, without the gift, how can they manifest it? They cannot.

And so, these walking after their own lusts have spent eighteen hundred years trying to convince us it CANNOT be manifest.

The Word of God says it can be, and that we should.

Remember that "Holy Ghost" is "pnuema hagion"

The text in Jude 1:20 reads "en pneumati agio proseuchomenoi," which is literally, "in spirit holy praying."

We are not told to build ourselves in our faith by praying for holy spirit to come, we already have the gift.

We build up ourselves by prayer via holy spirit. And what does the Word of God say prayer in holy spirit is?

Speaking in tongues.

If you want to build big beefy biceps, you pump dumbbells.

If you want to exercise your mind, you read, you do puzzles, you solve problems.

If you want to build yourself up spiritually, you speak in tongues. Then, in fellowship meetings, you speak in tongues and interpret what you have prayed.

You, "in holy spirit, pray."

Speaking in tongues is prayer, and it is what you can do to "exercise" the gift of God, the new spirit life that is in you.

God indeed answers prayers, even those we can't understand.

Then, as you seek to minister to the Body of Christ and to the carnal men and women lost in this world, get ready.

You are a spirit-filled creation, seeking to do your Father's will, and when God needs miracles, when He needs someone to do His will, who's He gonna call?

You.

As you read the Bible, look at each instance where believers speak in tongues, speak in the spirit, prophesy. What happened? Why?

Look at where revelation and visions are given. Are they word of knowledge, of wisdom? Are spirits discerned? How did God communicate these things?

Look at where miracles occur. Think of the faith God infuses the believer with to do this. Each character in Scripture was just a man, even the sinless man, Jesus Christ.

And so we leave this with you, O faithful in Christ.

We hope this series has helped you.

We pray that you think about all that which God has made available to you.

We know that God wants to fellowship with you as you with Him. That is a two-way street.

We know that Jesus Christ, Head of the Body, needs you to be his hands and feet to minister to his people. To minister to those who have pledged fealty to him, and to those injured on the sidelines, unsure of what they might do or be.

And we know that there is a dying world out there that needs the life that is in you.

Manifest that spirit life, shine it forth, for we are only here for a short while. The harvest is great, and the laborers few.

God bless you and keep you, above all, God be with you as you serve Him and obey His Will.

In the name of our Lord Jesus Christ, Amen.

Made in the USA
Coppell, TX
11 January 2022